D1132448

THE COMPLETE GUIDE TO NINE STAR KI

Please refer to this page when using Figures 5, 7, 11, 15 and 30.

To calculate your Nine Star Ki Birth Month Number see Figure 5 (page 17) and Figure 30 (page 177) using these column headings:

When your Nine Star Ki Birth Year Number is...	1, 4 or 7	2, 5 or 8	3, 6 or 9	For birthdays between

When referring to the Magic Square showing the houses and their transformation phases in Figure 7 (page 19) and Figure 11 (page 97) use this chart:

	SE	S	SW	
	House of **4** TREE	House of **9** FIRE	House of **2** EARTH	
E	House of **3** TREE	House of **5** EARTH	House of **7** METAL	W
	House of **8** EARTH	House of **1** WATER	House of **6** METAL	
	NE	N	NW	

When referring to the standard Five Transformation Chart showing elemental energetics in a relationship in Figure 15 (page 129) use this chart:

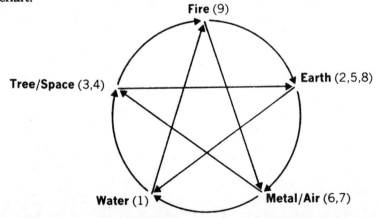

Fire (9)

Tree/Space (3,4)

Earth (2,5,8)

Water (1)

Metal/Air (6,7)

The Complete Guide to Nine Star Ki

Bob Sachs has studied Oriental disciplines for twenty years. He is a trained counsellor, holding a Master's Degree in Social Work (MSW), and works in New Mexico as a stress management and lifestyle consultant. He uses Nine Star Ki successfully for diagnosis and recommendation with both individuals and businesses.

Dear Ann,

May This inspire.

Yours,
Robert Sachs
Jan '99

The Complete Guide to
NINE STAR KI

A Timeless System for Discovering
Life, Love and Prosperity

◆

BOB SACHS

ELEMENT
Shaftesbury, Dorset ● Rockport, Massachusetts

Published in Great Britain in 1992 by
Element Books Limited
Longmead, Shaftesbury, Dorset

Published in the USA in 1992 by
Element, Inc
42 Broadway, Rockport, MA 01966

Cover illustration by Morag Charlton
Cover design by Barbara McGavin
Designed by Pete Russell, Faringdon, Oxfordshire
Typeset by Poole Typesetting (Wessex) Limited,
Fir Vale Road, Bournemouth, Dorset
Printed and bound in Great Britain by
Dotesios Ltd, Trowbridge, Wiltshire

British Library Cataloguing in Publication Data available

Library of Congress Cataloging in Publication Data available

ISBN 1–85230–334–4

Preface

Heather is an English school student. She is concerned about her final exams and where she should look for an adult career. Her family has expectations and plans regarding her future, but she feels drawn towards certain choices that are not in step with these expectations.

John is a university professor on sabbatical. He has decided to make some career changes, precipitated by an old interest and a desire to write. To initiate this transition he plans to travel. Yet, he is uncertain of what to do first and the right timing for the changes.

Mike and Sandra's marriage has been going sour for the last few years. Each feels pressured by the other and they feel as though they are on a merry-go-round of predictable situations and reactions. They do want to make things work, but Mike can't pull himself away from the feelings of an earlier divorce and custody battle. Sandra is torn between needing Mike for emotional support and wanting to establish a niche for herself through her work.

Denise is a supervisor in a hospital laboratory. She does not understand or get on with a number of her employees. She sees that changes need to be made, but feels confused about what steps she should take to create a more cohesive and productive staff team.

In all of these situations, Nine Star Ki offers clear guidance. There are, of course, many types of therapies and work strategies that can facilitate growth and change in the scenarios presented. However, few have a world view that is as embracing, dynamic and adaptable as Nine Star Ki (pronounced 'key').

That is my experience. As a social worker and a therapist I have examined numerous psychotherapeutic and management models. Each has offered me useful ideas and ways of handling the diversity of clients that I encounter. The Law of Five Transformations, the underpinning of oriental philosophy and healing, and Nine Star Ki in particular, however, give my practice a stronger organic base – something I can work out of that feels grounded, more balanced. My confidence in this model, in turn, is reflected in my clients, who feel this confidence and become inspired to tap into their own inherent abilities to learn for themselves from this model.

Individuals wanting to develop and grow, both in themselves and with others, therapists wanting to be more effective as agents of change, business-minded people wanting to make appropriate and timely business decisions – all will benefit from this book. Not acting from projection or cultural/habitual patterning, but from a living, vibrant truth of a basic kind, one's decisions and actions in the world become more efficient, productive, and self-empowering.

This is what this book offers.

There are many people that have helped in the production of this book. To all the ancient and modern sages adept in Nine Star Ki I am indebted. To teachers Michio Kushi and Rex Lassalle, many thanks. Much gratitude goes out to Colleen Reed, Wendy Buckles, Susan Biggs, artist Morag Charlton, Rebecca Wood and Judy Lawrence for technical assistance and advice. Many thanks to many others not named who showed confidence in and support for this project.

And an especial thank you to all who read this volume and find it useful in their lives.

Bob Sachs

Foreword

Nine Star Ki, or as it is known in Japan, *Kyu Sei Ki Gaku*, is a part of an ancient cosmology that was common to people throughout the world. It is based on understanding the way that yin and yang, or the two most basic forces in nature, interact to produce all changes in the universe. This universal cosmology, together with applications such as Nine Star Ki, developed at a time when people were living closer to the rhythms of nature and observing the Tao, or order of change, in their daily lives, including their way of eating. Their traditional diet of non-chemicalized whole grains, vegetables, beans and other natural foods enabled them to develop insight into the movement of life energy, or ki, in the planetary environment and in human affairs.

The ancient sages understood that despite what seems to be endless diversity, all things on earth and in heaven move and change in accordance with a simple order. Once this order is understood and confirmed in daily life, it becomes possible to know how future events are likely to unfold. It was through intuitive awareness of the law of change that the study of destiny – which represents the pinnacle of Oriental thinking and philosophy – was born.

Nine Star Ki, and Oriental Astrology in general, continues to be one of the most popular subjects presented in our macrobiotic seminars around the world. Thousands of people have studied Oriental Astrology and have found it to be a useful and practical guide to understanding human relationships, personal health, current events, and human destiny in general. It offers everyone a compass for navigating the troubled waters of modern times.

The Complete Guide to Nine Star Ki is a most welcome and useful Nine Star Ki sourcebook, shedding further light on the personality types of the Nine Ki characters as well as being excellent in its analysis of the interactions between the numbers that make up human personalities. This book and our new introductory book, *Nine Star Ki*, provide readers with the opportunity to discover how the principles of Oriental Astrology apply to their daily lives.

In closing, we would like to thank Bob Sachs for his effort in compiling this book and for making this practical and useful knowledge available to people in the modern world.

MICHIO KUSHI
East West Foundation, founder
EDWARD ESKO
Kushi Institute, Counsellor

To Michio Kushi,
who opened my eyes to the depth, beauty, and power
of worlds seen and unseen through his knowledge,
patience and kindness.

To friend Rex Lassalle,
who prodded me on in the study of Nine Star Ki
and the empowerment of myself.

To my beloved life companion, Melanie,
who has always been there to support
me in our us-ness.

To my children, Kai, Tina and Jabeth,
who cheered when the book was finished.

May all beings who are touched by this book
find it beneficial.

Contents

List of Figures

How to Use This Book

This section is provided for your convenience. Although it will take you a short time to learn how to make Nine Star Ki calculations, the following steps will help you to use the book immediately. They can also serve as a reminder while you perfect your calculation skills.

1. Establish the month, day and year of birth of the person on whom you would like to do a Nine Star Ki evaluation. You do *not* need the exact time or location of birth.

2. The years and months of the Nine Star Ki system are in accordance with the Chinese calendar. Thus the beginning of the year is in early February. Looking at the year chart (Figure 4) on page 14, find the Nine Star Ki number associated with the year of birth. Anyone born between 1 January and 4 February should take the number from the previous year (for example, a person born on 6 January 1947 should consider their year to be 1946 and therefore look at the Nine Star Ki number associated with 1946). The year number is referred to in the text as the adult natal or adult natal year number. This number is associated with your greatest potential for growth and development. Read the description of this number in Part 2 of the book.

3. Look for the number associated with the month and day of birth in Figure 5 on page 17. This is called the child natal or child natal month number. This number is associated with your upbringing and your reactions to outside influences during earlier years, hence your conditioning, socially, physically and emotionally. Apart from its influence on the first eighteen years of life, this number's traits become active in later years when under stress. Traits of the month can be more easily taxed if they are over-emphasized. Read the description of this number in Part 2 of the book.

4. The adult and child natal numbers together are the most significant part of the Nine Star Ki chart. There are relationships between these numbers that influence your behaviour, health and relationships. Figure 10 on page 25 will help you to find important passages in the text which are relevant to the adult-child number configuration you are examining. Read these passages.

5. Take time to reflect on the material. How much do you respond from your adult natal or child natal number? In what circumstances? Be open. Be accepting.

Part I

♦

INTRODUCTION

♦

Humankind in Time and Space

◆ From Tortoise Shell to Lamaistic Calendars

Two thousand years before the Common Era, a series of floods threatened civilization along the Yellow River in China. A man of extraordinary talents, Wu of Hsia, appeared at this time, through his knowledge of rivers and engineering, improved the movement of the river, re-establishing order to the region. For this he was made emperor, and prosperity increased for all.

When making his river improvements, Wu came across a tortoise, symbol of long life and happiness. He was overjoyed to have this tortoise, especially as it was said that divine force lived in the shell of turtles.

Upon closer inspection, Wu noticed unusual white and black markings on the shell. These markings varied in their position and number, creating what were to be called Nine Chambers; each chamber contained a certain number of black or white markings. Seeing these as a divine sign, Wu of Hsia decided that a theory should be developed about their significance and how they applied to nature and human action. Consulting with his sages, he constructed a theory using the tortoise shell markings as a focal point for organizing all other systems of knowledge.[1]

Once one goes beyond this legendary origin, experts do not agree on what comes next in what Chinese called *Chiu Kung Ming Li* or Nine Star Astrology. W. K. Chu and W. A. Sherrill contend that the nine chambers were the basis for the Later Heaven

Sequence or Lo Map, a map symbolically representing the inter-action of humankind, nature, and celestial influences. The Lo Map is the basis for Chinese geomancy (*Feng Shui*) or the art of placement, and directionology or considerations for movement and travel. The Lo Map is also considered the origin of the *Lo Shu* or Magic Square, the symbology used in Nine Star Ki astrology.[2]

The exact – or even approximate – dates of the initial utilization of the Lo Map and *Lo Shu* for geomancy, directionology and prediction remain obscure. However, it is known that the Sung Almanacs, dated to the tenth century CE contain fragments of Magic Squares and have been deciphered to reveal an elaborate system of numerology practised at that time. These almanacs were found in the ruins of lamaistic monasteries in the Tun Huang region of China, thus revealing the links between Tibetan and Chinese utilization of this system.[3] The proliferation of these practices, including Nine Star Ki, to Japan and other regions of the Far East remains a mystery. More than likely, with ordinary commerce and trade, travellers shared their knowledge and beliefs. Such sharing, combined with our human curiosity, has undoubtedly contributed to a richer body of knowledge of life that cannot be credited to any one culture.

◆ An Ancient System of Astrology for Modern Times

At a time when humankind was more keenly aware of its intimate relationship with nature than it is today, astrology was a part of life. Life situations, crises and opportunities for material and spiritual growth could be perceived and acted upon more clearly as the interaction between microcosm (humankind) and macro-cosm (heaven and earth) was revealed by those adept in this ancient science.

If such information was useful to societies that lived closer to nature, it is even more vital today when the pace and stimulation of modern living makes us lose touch with what truly keeps us alive and gives life meaning. And while every system of astrology has something to offer us, the calculations and information available in Nine Star Ki Astrology are relatively easy to learn, thus making it a system suited to modern times and our way of life.

The same applies to the theory supporting Nine Star Ki. Some may want a scholarly approach to this theory, in which case Appendix 2 will be interesting and informative. For those of you wanting key concepts so that you can just get on and work with the Ki, the following definitions will suffice for interpreting the basic data of the Nine Star Ki archetypes.

Yin, Yang and Ki

Yin and *yang* are the names given to polar opposite forces in nature. Considered to be *the* primal forces from which everything is created and dissolved or destroyed, each is ascribed certain properties, properties that remain constant even though different oriental traditions will use the terms yin and yang in opposing ways. The properties associated with these two terms in this volume are in keeping with those of oriental philosopher George Ohsawa and the Macrobiotic tradition.

The distinctions drawn between yin and yang can be seen in Ohsawa's classification of their traits and tendencies.[4]

	Yin	Yang
tendency	expansion	contraction
position	outward	inward
structure	space	time
direction	ascent	descent
colour	purple	red
temperature	cold	hot
weight	light	heavy
catalyst	water	fire
atomic particle	electron	proton
light	dark	bright
vibration	short wave	long wave
work	psychological	physical
attitude	gentle, negative	active, positive
biological	vegetable	animal
sex	female	male
nerves	orthosympathetic	parasympathetic
elements	K,O,P,Ca,N	H,As,Cl, Na,C

Figure 1. Yin and yang traits and tendencies

On a more psycho-spiritual level, yin is classified as intuitive awareness and compassion. The Chinese deity Kuan Yin best exemplifies this. Yang is classified as intellect with the will towards action. Even though such distinctions are drawn, it must be understood that yin does not exist without yang or vice versa. Both are present and needed in varying degrees for all things in nature – whether they be rocks or thought forms – to exist.

Ki refers to life force. This life force is present in the interaction between yin and yang. It is only detected by its presence in this interaction. Yet to say that it is the same as yin and yang would not be correct. The cultivation and direction of ki or life force is the primary purpose of the meditative, healing and martial arts traditions of the orient. Still, like life itself, it escapes the scrutiny of the question, 'Why?' However, the question, 'How?' is permissible and thus creates opportunities for study and mastery.

The Five Transformations

As the forces of yin, yang and ki interact in varying degrees, specific phases are created through which all things must pass. Sages observed five distinct phases in the cycle from birth to death. These are *creation, gestation, maturation, full maturation*, or *completion*, then *dormancy* or *dissolution*. An example of this is a seed which sprouts, grows, matures into a fruit, reaches full ripening and then falls to the ground, from whence the cycle is repeated. All things in nature, from the most inert (minerals) to the most subtle (thought vibration) go through all five phases. Not only that, sages could see sub-cycles in each phase. So for example in the case of a piece of fruit, the seed has to mature and decay before the sprout can emerge, and so on.

The ancients observed that in each phase, regardless of whether it is a part of a long or a brief cycle, there are distinct properties inherent in it. Over time, the aggregates of a certain phase were given names that metaphorically symbolize the dynamics of that phase.

1. The energetics and properties present in birth, creation, or first impulse are known as *tree* or *space*. Tree implies something breaking through the ground for the first time, arising from dormancy. Space implies the invisible potential from which all things are born.

2. The energetics and properties present in gestation are known as *fire*. Fire implies something raging with potential, like food that is cooking but not yet done. This is the phase that is most outwardly active – as if everything is being worked on all at once. Fire is very consuming and noticeable from afar.

3. The energetics and properties present in maturation are known as *earth*. Earth implies consolidation, where things are settling down from fire. Things are seen in their entirety – the first glimpses of a finished product. Earth bears the quality of accomplishment.

4. The energetics and properties present in completion or full maturation are known as *air* or *metal*. All living organisms need air to maintain life. When something has reached its ripest, it has reached its capacity. In a living organism, this means that the level of air that it is consuming is likewise at full capacity. Beyond this point it will begin to lose its capacity and its use of air will likewise diminish. Metal implies maximum solidity. There is a quality here of boldness.

5. The energetics and properties present in dormancy or dissolution are referred to as *water*. Water implies dissolution, where life recedes to a point where it can rest as potential.

This can be summarized as follows:

Phases in the Birth to Death Cycle	The Elements
Creation	Tree/Space
Gestation	Fire
Maturation	Earth
Completion	Air/Metal
Dissolution	Water

Figure 2. Elements associated with phases in the birth to death cycle

Sages called these the *elements* of life. However, because elements to us implies irreducible building blocks like in our atomic chart, modern theorists of oriental knowledge have elected to use the word *transformation* to convey the irreducible yet *dynamic* nature of each phase and its characteristics.

Thus all things in nature possess the Five Transformations. Different species are dominated by different transformations and even within one species, the blending of transformations varies with time and circumstances. Relating this to human life, we are born and eventually die, in which case all transformations show themselves in the grand life cycle. But even daily, cells in different organs and tissues are born and die. Some of these changes are by genetic design; some are dramatically influenced by how we live. And sages could see the Five Transformations at work on the physiological, psychological and spiritual dimensions of our being. Some of their findings and classifications are found on the chart in Appendix 1. For further information on this subject, see Appendix 2.

◆ Nine Star Ki Astrology: Learning from Cycles in Nature

Wise people of the past who fully comprehended the relationship between heaven, earth and mankind observed that every nine years there is a predictable cycle in which each transformation becomes dominant for a given period of time. The chart in Figure 3 shows the relationship between the number of the year in the nine-year cycle and the transformation most dominant at that time. (The chart also shows whether a year and its associated transformation are considered more yin or yang at that time, and the trigrams that came from the encoding first found on Wu of Hsia's tortoise.)

These people also observed monthly, daily and hourly cycles. Thus the nine-year relationship to the transformations was similarly reflected in smaller increments of time.

By virtue of the time that we are born, certain transformations are more dominant in our nature than others. All the descriptions of the numbers and the transformations they represent that follow in these pages are based on centuries of observing human life and behaviour. And as will be seen, the sages were able to look into the deepest aspects of our being and see the subtle

Transformation Phase (Element)	Ying/Yang	Number	Trigram
Fire	Yin	9	☲ (Li)
Earth	Yang	8	☶ (Ken)
Air/Metal	Yin	7	☱ (Tui)
Air/Metal	Yang	6	☰ Ch'ien)
Earth	Yin/Yang	5	none
Tree/Space	Yin	4	☴ (Sun)
Tree/Space	Yang	3	☳ (Chen)
Earth	Yin	2	☷ (K'un)
Water	Yang	1	☵ (K'an)

Figure 3. The relationship between year number and transformation phase

influences of the Five Transformations in our likes, dislikes, personality quirks, interactive skills and aspirations. Further information on this subject is provided in Appendix 2.

Of What Use is Nine Star Ki in my Life?

Nine Star Ki is a very versatile and accessible astrological system. And what makes this book *The Complete Guide to Nine Star Ki* a unique volume on this system is that along with useful personal information for understanding ourselves and others, equal attention is given to understanding the processes of interaction, the dynamics between people.

People can approach it from a variety of levels, from personal to professional.

1. For those with a personal interest, there are four basic relationships addressed. First and foremost is one's relationship to oneself. For self-growth and development, Nine Star Ki will reveal to you your *core* or primary strengths and weaknesses on physical, psychological and spiritual levels. Knowing what your primary strengths are, you can tap into them, aligning the three other relationship areas of intimacy with others, work or business, and spiritual development for greater fulfilment. Knowing your weaknesses, rather than berating yourself for character defects, you will understand – on an energetic level – what you need to cultivate in your character and being. As regards prediction, you will – with practice – understand why certain years and months affect you the way they do, thus enabling you to plan careers, holidays, or any other form of life change, with a greater sense of focus and purpose. And your ability to understand and communicate effectively with others will be greatly enhanced as your perception becomes more aligned with how things really are for you rather than how you have been conditioned to see yourself and others.

2. *If you are a therapist or agent of change for others* (including doctors, lawyers, etc.), you will find in Nine Star Ki an excellent short cut to understanding the people you counsel. Knowing a person's elemental influence and addressing them accordingly will create a stronger bond and enhance communication and transformative processes and techniques on all levels. An entire section of this book is devoted to the application of Nine Star Ki to group dynamics. Thus working with family systems and structured groups in any context will be more realistic and accurate. You will be more effective in facilitating change and growth on personal and interpersonal levels. Consequently you will save time and find your work less stressful and more rewarding.

3. *Businesses and business-minded people* will learn how to bring out the best in themselves and others, such as employees. You will understand what makes any kind of team or organization function the way it does. You will be able to select the right person for the right job, delegate more effectively, and determine what traits in an organization need to be cultivated for greater effectiveness, productivity and growth.

The next chapter is a description of how to calculate the year and month Nine Star Ki numbers that are relevant to you, what can be learned from understanding the transformation phases that are associated with them, and how to interpret the various combinations of year and month Nine Star Ki numbers that are created at the time of birth and over the passage of time. This knowledge can then be applied to yourself for your own growth and development, for understanding and nurturing others, and for working more effectively in any group situation.

Ki as used in this book refers to energy – life energy. As it is pronounced 'key', there is an obvious, even deeper meaning to the title. *Life is energy in transformation.* If one can learn the mechanisms underlying this transformational process, one indeed has the 'key' to a deeper, fuller, richer life.

How to Calculate Your Nine Star Ki Numbers

Although there are both hourly and daily times in which one of the five transformations is dominant, in order to focus on more basic constitutional or long-lasting traits and conditional or circumstantial tendencies we shall focus only on the Nine-Star Ki numbers and associated transformations connected with a person's birth year and month. The descriptions of the Nine Numbers in Part 2 are used for understanding both natal year and natal month tendencies. However, there is a significant difference in how the year and month numbers impact our lives. This follows in the description of how to calculate both of these numbers.

◆ Calculating Your Adult Natal Year Number

The number and transformation phase ascribed to a person's year of birth has to do with their optimal potential. As a person becomes an individual in their own right, the qualities of the natal year become more and more apparent in their physical expression, attitudes and actions. The emphasis here is on strengths. This does not mean that there are no challenges in the person's life, paradoxes in the personality, conflicts, and such like. Rather, when a person begins to actualize their natal year potential fully the seeming quirks characteristic of that year and resulting interactions with life's events become the texture that makes their life interesting and fruitful. To distinguish these year traits from month traits, they are classified as 'adult' traits or potentials as opposed to the month influence which is classified as 'child' traits or potentials. (You should get used to seeing year traits described as 'adult natal year' traits and month traits as 'child natal month' traits.)

The natal year is about self-actualization. Therefore it is not something one just falls into easily. Indeed conditional patterns from childhood and circumstances may prevail and the adult natal year potential remain dormant. To overcome these limitations on one's potential requires personal commitment to openness and growth.

A list of the numbers associated with particular years is given in Figure 4. Please bear in mind that the year is based on the Chinese lunar calendar. This means that the year begins roughly on 4 February. Thus if you were born between 1 January and February 3, use the preceding year as the way to find your associated adult natal year.

Of course, once you become proficient in knowing the traits of the transformations, you may want to calculate the numbers without the use of the chart. To do so, there is a formula to work to.

Let's take an example: 1947. To get the Nine Star Ki number for the year 1947, take the last two digits (4 and 7) and add them together: $4 + 7 = 11$. Now add the two digits of the number 11 together $(1 + 1)$ and you get the number 2. This 2 is then subtracted from the number 10. The answer is 8. This is the Nine Star Ki number for 1947. Simply stated, you take the last two digits of the year in which you were born and add them together until they are reduced to a single digit (1–9). This single digit is then subtracted from the number 10, giving you the Nine Star Ki number for that year.

Another example could be 1960: $6 + 0 = 6$, $10 - 6 = 4$. This is the Nine Star Ki number for the year 1960.

This formula only works for this century (1901–99) and would need to be modified when entering into the twenty-first century (see Appendix 6). But remember that if you were born between 1 January and 3 February of a given year, your Nine Star Ki year number would be that of the previous calendar year. For example, if your date of birth is 15 January 1971, you would not

Year	Number	Year	Number	Year	Number	Year	Number
1896	5	1925	3	1954	1	1983	8
1897	4	1926	2	1955	9	1984	7
1898	3	1927	1	1956	8	1985	6
1899	2	1928	9	1957	7	1986	5
1900	1	1929	8	1958	6	1987	4
1901	9	1930	7	1959	5	1988	3
1902	8	1931	6	1960	4	1989	2
1903	7	1932	5	1961	3	1990	1
1904	6	1933	4	1962	2	1991	9
1905	5	1934	3	1963	1	1992	8
1906	4	1935	2	1964	9	1993	7
1907	3	1936	1	1965	8	1994	6
1908	2	1937	9	1966	7	1995	5
1909	1	1938	8	1967	6	1996	4
1910	9	1939	7	1968	5	1997	3
1911	8	1940	6	1969	4	1998	2
1912	7	1941	5	1970	3	1999	1
1913	6	1942	4	1971	2	2000	9
1914	5	1943	3	1972	1	2001	8
1915	4	1944	2	1973	9	2002	7
1916	3	1945	1	1974	8	2003	6
1917	2	1946	9	1975	7	2004	5
1918	1	1947	8	1976	6	2005	4
1919	9	1948	7	1977	5	2006	3
1920	8	1949	6	1978	4	2007	2
1921	7	1950	5	1979	3	2008	1
1922	6	1951	4	1980	2	2009	9
1923	5	1952	3	1981	1	2010	8
1924	4	1953	2	1982	9	2011	7

Figure 4. Year and the yang, or descending, natal year numbers

calculate your Nine Star Ki year number on 1971, but on 1970 $(7+0=7, 10-7=3)$.

For those of you not using a formula for the nineteenth or twenty-first century calculations, note that for the time before 1901 and after 1999, the number of the year in the nine-year cycle follows in a sequence from 9 down to 1 and then back to 9 again. That is, 1999 will be a 1 year and the year 2000 will be a 9 year, 2001 will be 8, and so on.

Oriental masters observed that there are both descending and ascending numbers through time. The descending or yang order shown here is the one most commonly used. Appendix 4 explains the significance of the ascending order along with useful charts for both years and months.

◆ Calculating Your Child Natal Month Number

The number and transformation phase ascribed to a person's month of birth has similar potential to the natal year, but is more bound by time and conditioned by events. It is in the first two cycles of nine – up to the age of eighteen years – that the natal month's transformation phase is most noticeably dominant, that is when a person is more dependent upon others and has less obvious control over their circumstances. Thus reactions and responses to others and to events are determined by the qualities and characteristics of the natal month's transformation phase.

It is also the foundation from which the potentials of a person's natal year will emerge. Consequently the transition from natal month to natal year aspects can vary considerably – smooth, rocky, chaotic, etc. This is not only because of the reactions and responses a person has gone through in dealing with others and with circumstances. There are also definite ways in which two transformation phases interact with each other, in which case what the person experiences in going from a more dependent to independent way of life and being may be strictly an internal (psychological) process.

In times of stress in adult years, responses and reactions of the natal month will re-emerge. This can also happen if, in early years, because of particular circumstances, usually crises and traumatic events, a person was thrust into a more independent, hence a more adult, mode. In such a case the adult year characteristics may dominate the child month characteristics in an unhealthy way, and it is only logical that they should re-emerge when there is no crisis. This may, in fact, be the origin of the adult-child response, and what is actually referred to as the 'child within' in literature on co-dependency and dysfunctional families. Another circumstance in which the natal month qualities may re-emerge in later years is when a person is in a position where they may again become dependent upon others.

When the natal month's transformation phase and its associated organs, systems, etc. are reactivated in this manner, it usually becomes the ground for physiological and psychological stress and disease. Rarely do the bodily systems, organs or psychological functions associated with the natal year become over-stressed or diseased, unless there are external pressures or life-threatening situations arising from outside causes. In general, and more often than not, when a person finds that their natal month transformation is being reactivated, along with it come unresolved childhood patterns and reactions. Once again perceiving ourselves to be victims of circumstances, we lose our ability to express ourselves and open the door to any number of problems in the many aspects of our lives.

The remedy for such a turn of events is to acknowledge the situation, that we are in our natal month expression, look for ways that would help us to develop or bring such a phase to a positive resolution, and move on. The strategies to make a transition from natal month (child) to natal year (adult) expression are numerous. The key ingredients for a successful blend, where both child and adult aspects are being nurtured in a balanced fashion, are kindness to oneself and humour.

There is no simple formula for calculating the natal month number, so a chart is provided below.

It should be noted that while monthly charts from both the Chinese and Japanese systems appear to give similar beginning and ending dates for the months, those persons whose birthdays fall on the date at the beginning or end of a month, or one day before or after that date, should look to the transformation phase ascribed to the two months meeting at that time to determine which characteristics seem most appropriate for them. For example, if a person is born on 7 August in a 1 year, they should look at the characteristics ascribed to both 3 and 2 natal numbers.

Although this is the chart we refer to generally, as it divides the year into twelve equal portions and ascribes numbers accordingly, Sherrill and Chu's monthly chart in *An Anthology of I Ching* is based on the Chinese system of twenty-four seasons. An explanation for this variation and the chart itself can be found in Appendix 3.

Figure 5. Months and the yang, or descending, natal month numbers

When your Nine Star Ki Birth Year Number is . . .	1, 4, or 7	2, 5, or 8	3, 6, or 9	For birthdays between
Your Nine Star Ki Birth Month Number is . . .	8	2	5	4 Feb–5 Mar
	7	1	4	6 Mar–4 Apr
	6	9	3	5 Apr–5 May
	5	8	2	6 May–5 Jun
	4	7	1	6 Jun–7 Jul
	3	6	9	8 Jul–7 Aug
	2	5	8	8 Aug–7 Sep
	1	4	7	8 Sep–8 Oct
	9	3	6	9 Oct–7 Nov
	8	2	5	8 Nov–7 Dec
	7	1	4	8 Dec–5 Jan
	6	9	3	6 Jan–3 Feb

◆ The Gender of the Number

We saw previously that each number has associated with it a transformation and that each transformation is proportionately more yin or yang in its properties, relatively speaking. Some transformations are more dominantly yin or yang, and others have combinations of yin and yang that vary in accordance with time – again, relatively speaking. Thus, for example, whereas fire is associated with yin and water with yang, earth, tree/space, and metal/air have both more overtly yin and yang aspects. Thus one finds that in the passage of time, numbers associated with one element (such as tree/space) will have a yang (3) and yin (4) period of time.

The yin and yang nature of each of the numbers is significant for personality characteristics and physiological/psychological tendencies. Thus, using the concept of female (f) as representing yin and male (m) as representing yang, each number when calculated is listed with its yin or yang aspect by putting an 'f' or 'm' beside it. Thus a person born in a 1 Water year will see it represented as 1(m), the 'm' representing male or yang, whereas in 7(f), the 'f' would signify female or yin.

These gender aspects to the numbers *do not vary* according to whether the person is male or female. They remain constant and there is some significance in there being a dominant male or female energetic in the numbers for a man or a woman. Classical acupuncture theory classifies yin and yang as having certain archetypal characteristics. The polarity of these two is often described in terms of gender. Such categorization is not accidental or arbitrary. The deeper significance of this gender distinction is discussed at length in Part 3.

◆ The House of the Child Natal Month Number

Similar to occidental and other oriental astrologies, the Nine Star Ki system includes the notion of 'houses'. These houses arise from the concepts inherent in what is called the Magic Square. Simply stated, the Magic Square represents the qualities, order and movement of all phenomena here on earth as expressed in the Law of Five Transformations.

Figure 6. The Magic Square (*Lo Shu*)

	SE	S	SW
	4	9	2
E	3	5	7	W
	8	1	6	
	NE	N	NW

Figure 6 is the classic Magic Square as traditionally depicted. What makes the square 'magic' is that with 5 in the middle, if you take any three numbers in a row in any direction within the square, they will add up to 15. The numbers as they are represented in this square with 5 in the middle is the standard representation. Thus not only are the numbers in their traditional positions, the number in each one of the square's positions is the house number of that position. (Figure 7.)

SE   S   SW

House of **4** TREE	House of **9** FIRE	Houseof **2** EARTH
House of **3** TREE	House of **5** FIRE	House of **7** EARTH
House of **8** TREE	House of **1** FIRE	House of **6** EARTH

Figure 7. The Magic Square showing the houses and their transformation phases

E   W

NE   N   NW

The Magic Square or *Lo Shu* was also given an octagonal or eight-sided appearance as well, known in Yoshikawa's *The Ki* as the Universal Chart. Because both representations are useful, I will use both, as they are both easy to comprehend and work with, and it will accustom you to using both.

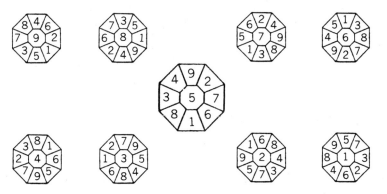

Figure 8. Universal Charts

Each year and month, the number in the centre of the Magic' Square changes to the natal number of the year or month. Thus in a 9 year, 9 is in the centre; in an 8 year, 8 is in the centre, and so on. When this happens, all the other numbers migrate or change position in the Magic Square. Figure 8, showing the octagonal versions of the Magic Square, indicates what numbers are where when the number in the centre changes.

Although the numbers change their positions over time, the houses remain the same. Thus as each number and its associated transformation phase enter a particular house, there is an interaction that takes place between the basic qualities of the number entering that house and the house itself. Please bear in mind that the term 'house' as used in Nine Star Ki should not be equated in any way with the 'ninth house' or 'tenth house' etc. as referred to in Western astrology. The only similarity is in the term.

Every person's birth (natal) year is located in the house of 5 at the time of their birth and every nine years after that. To determine the house of the natal month, one needs to find where the natal month number is situated when the person's natal year is in the middle of the Magic Square.

Here is an example. A man is born on 1 March 1957. The natal year number for 1957 is 7 and the natal month number is 8. If you refer to Figure 9, you will see that when 7 is in the centre (where 5 was originally), 8 is in the position where 6 was. So 7 is said to be in the house of 5, and 8 in the house of 6.

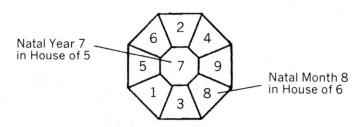

Figure 9. Chart for someone born on 1 March 1957.

◆ Writing Down Your Complete Birthdate in Nine Star Ki Configuration

If we were to take our previous example of a man born on 1 March 1957 and write out the Nine Star Ki numbers, it would appear as follows:

Year	Month	House
7*f*	(8*m*)	six*m*

Because the yin or yang nature of each of the numbers is significant for personality characteristics and physiological/psychological tendencies, using the concept of female (*f*) as representing yin and male (*m*) as representing yang, the birth-date can be written in the following manner:

7*f* (8*m*) six*m*

Figure 3 on page 9 will help you become familiar with which numbers are female (yin) and male (yang).

Familiarize yourself with writing out Nine Star Ki birth numbers in the manner shown. In this way, you can create constant birth-date charts that are immediately understood by those studying and using the Nine Star Ki system.

When the numbers are written in this manner, the following questions can be considered regarding the person being analyzed. Using our example of 7*f*(8*m*)six*m*:

1. What are the characteristics of the natal year, 7?

2. What are the characteristics of the natal month, 8?

3. What is the relationship between the transformation phases of the natal year, 7, and the natal month, 8?

4. What dynamic is in operation with the natal month, 8, being in the house of 6 at the time of birth?

5. What significance does the gender *f* or *m* for the natal year, 7*f* and natal month 8*m* have for the gender and sexual identity of the given person?

To make such an investigation easier, there is an Easy Reference Table at the end of this chapter to enable you to find the pages in the text which will help you answer these questions.

These are the basic questions for which the profiles, narratives and descriptions of numbers, house and gender dynamics in Part 2 have been designed. With greater proficiency in this system and deeper understanding of the Law of Five Transformations, you will be able to understand your changes and experiences, and those of other people, as the numbers migrate into the various houses during the months and years. Consequently, knowledge gleaned of yourself, of others and of relationships is not static but dynamic. Nature, in accordance with the Law of Five Transformations, provides us with a rich and varied assortment of elemental and energetic experiences from which we can learn of the mystery of life.

◆ Systems of Knowledge and Art

Systems of knowledge, be they analytically based sciences, philosophical theories or spiritual awarenesses derived from various methodologies, become meaningful only in so far as we are able to integrate them into our lives. Meaning is a very private matter and how we derive meaning from our world of experiences is based on factors too numerous or mysterious for any one book to expound fully. In many ways, the inferences and conclusions we draw from our lives – even if those inferences and conclusions seem to be based on 'hard' facts – are woven together like a unique tapestry, a piece of art.

Intuited knowledge and data drawn from an awareness of energetics as is found in the I Ching, Law of Five Transformations and Nine Star Ki may not bear the scrutiny of the scientific methods we currently apply. Indeed the language of such knowledge and data is often a mixture of philosophy, psychology, religion, natural science and metaphor. In fact, it is often the use of metaphor which creates the glue to enable such a variety of concepts to hang together.

Metaphors also create pictures of broader aspects of reality that we may not be able to conceptualize or describe in any other way. We should therefore also not be surprised that in the process of piecing data together contradictions arise within the picture. Unless we are robots, there are bound to be contradictions and inconsistencies in our approaches even to the same situations. This may have more to do with elemental and dynamic processes inherent in our nature than some kind of pathological aberration or sign of being weak-willed. It can be tremendously liberating and empowering to embrace our quirks and contradictory ways.

Thus it is that what is presented as Nine Star Ki data is a blend of knowledge and art, where the colours and textures of data and knowledge gleaned from the I Ching and Law of Five Transformations are pieced together with the glue of metaphor born of intuition and personal experience. In addition to studying the text, you can deepen your knowledge of the Law of Five Transformations by reading Naboru Muramoto's *Healing Ourselves* and William Tara's *Macrobiotics and Human Behavior*. At the same time you are advised to test what is presented by reflecting upon your own experiences of life. In this way, what is studied becomes more meaningful. It also creates the possibility of new linkages within the body of knowledge and data being discovered, thus benefiting oneself and others.

◆ A Brief Word or Two about Attitude

To see ourselves truly as we are, we must learn to relax and give up our concern about who we are. We are used to typecasting ourselves or living in the images that others have created for us. Although we think that we are being free in our choices, we are too often bound by the cultural and social concepts of the day. The power of Nine Star Ki is that the traits and characteristics presented come from an ancient tradition based on the deepest contemplations and meditations of the great sages of the past. This makes such a body of knowledge and data more likely to cut through cultural and social nuances and be more precise and time tested. Therefore it speaks to us more directly, in a way that feels more truthful. It may also be an affront to the person we have portrayed ourselves to be.

As mentioned in the previous section, we need to reflect on what the Nine Star Ki presents to us. Reflection does not mean, however, to dissect our experience and the data morbidly. Reflection requires an ability to see things as they are. To do this, we need openness and humour. Reflection without openness and humour would lead us down a path where we become straitjacketed by our limited perceptions, with anything which does not fit within our perceptions being viewed with some level of cynicism.

Not to reflect at all and just to accept the Nine Star Ki without personal scrutiny would make us mindless devotees.

The value of Nine Star Ki is its usefulnes in helping us to deepen our appreciation of who we are and the transformations we go through in life. It should not be used as a new toy or gimmick to replace truly felt emotion or insight. In that way, Nine-Star Ki becomes a facilitating tool rather than an answer to life and living in the world.

Figure 10. Easy-Reference Table. Once you have calculated the Nine Star Ki numbers for a given birth-date, locate that combination in the left-hand column of the table. Reading from left to right on the same line, you will find crosses in at least four columns. Besides the number narratives, these indicate other significant points for the given number combination. Refer to the page number at the top of the column to find the information in the text.

Nine Star Ki Number	Adult number page	Child number page	Child number is mother to house it resides in (p.105)	Child number is son to house it resides in (p.106)	Child number is in house that it controls (p.106)	Child number is in house that it is controlled by (p.107)	Child number resides in house of same transformation as itself (p.108)	Adult number supports child number (p.117)	Adult number controls child number (p.117)	Child number supports adult (p.116)	Child number controls adult number (p.118)	Adult and child number are same (p.107)	Adult and child transformation (not number) are same (p.118)	Males Same/same (p.121)	Males Same/opposite (p.121)	Males Opposite/same (p.122)	Males Opposite/opposite (p.122)	Females Same/same (p.121)	Females Same/opposite (p.121)	Females Opposite/same (p.122)	Females Opposite/opposite (p.122)
1m(1m) five m/f	87	87				•						•		•							•
1m(2f) six m	87	80	•								•				•					•	
1m(3m) seven f	87	72				•		•						•							•
1m(4f) eight m	87	64			•			•							•					•	
1m(5m/f) nine f	87	57		•							•			•	•					•	•
1m(6m) one m	87	51	•							•				•							•
1m(7f) two f	87	44		•						•					•					•	
1m(8m) three m	87	39				•					•			•							•
1m(9f) four f	87	33		•					•						•					•	
2f(1m) four f	80	87	•						•							•		•			
2f(2f) five m/f	80	80					•	•								•	•	•			
2f(3m) six m	80	72				•			•							•		•			
2f(4f) seven f	80	64				•			•							•	•	•			
2f(5m/f) eight m	80	57				•							•			•	•	•	•		
2f(6m) nine f	80	51				•	•									•		•			
2f(7f) one m	80	44	•				•									•	•	•			
2f(8m) two f	80	39					•						•			•		•			
2f(9m) three m	80	33		•					•							•	•	•			
3m(1m) three m	72	87	•						•					•							•
3m(2f) four f	72	80				•		•							•					•	
3m(3m) five m/f	72	72			•					•				•							•
3m(4f) six m	72	64				•					•				•					•	
3m(5m/f) seven f	72	57	•					•						•	•					•	•
3m(6m) eight m	72	51		•						•				•							•
3m(7f) nine f	72	44				•			•						•					•	
3m(8m) one m	72	39			•			•						•							•
3m(9m) two m	72	33	•				•								•					•	
4f(1m) two f	64	87				•			•							•		•			
4f(2f) three m	64	80				•		•									•	•	•		

Nine Star Ki Number	Adult number page	Child number page	Child number is mother to house it resides in (p.105)	Child number is son to house it resides in (p.106)	Child number is in house that it controls (p.106)	Child number is in house that it is controlled by (p.107)	Child number resides in house of same transformation as itself (p.108)	Adult number supports child number (p.117)	Adult number controls child number (p.117)	Child number supports adult (p.116)	Child number controls adult number (p.118)	Adult and child number are same (p.107)	Adult and child transformation (not number) are same (p.118)	Males Same/same (p.121)	Males Same/opposite (p.121)	Males Opposite/same (p.122)	Males Opposite/opposite (p.122)	Females Same/same (p.121)	Females Same/opposite (p.121)	Females Opposite/same (p.122)	Females Opposite/opposite (p.122)
4f(3m) four f	64	72					•						•			•			•		
4f(4f) five m/f	64	64		•						•						•	•	•			
4f(5m/f) six m	64	57	•					•								•	•	•			
4f(6m) seven f	64	51					•			•						•		•			
4f(7f) eight m	64	44		•						•						•	•	•			
4f(8m) nine f	64	39		•			•									•		•			
4f(9f) one m	64	33				•		•								•	•	•			
5m/f(1m) one m	57	87					•	•						•		•			•		•
5m/f(2f) two f	57	80					•						•	•	•	•		•		•	
5m/f(3m) three m	57	72					•			•				•		•		•			•
5m/f(4f) four f	57	64					•			•						•	•	•		•	
5m/f(5m/f) five m/f	57	57					•						•	•	•	•	•	•	•	•	•
5m/f(6m) six m	57	51					•	•						•		•		•			•
5m/f(7f) seven f	57	44					•	•								•	•	•		•	
5m/f(8m) eight m	57	39					•					•		•		•		•		•	
5m/f(9f) nine f	57	33					•			•						•	•	•		•	
6m(1m) nine f	51	87		•				•						•							•
6m(2f) one m	51	80		•					•							•				•	
6m(3m) two f	51	72		•					•					•							•
6m(4f) three m	51	64					•	•								•				•	
6m(5m/f) four f	51	57				•			•					•	•					•	•
6m(6m) five m/f	51	51		•								•		•							•
6m(7f) six m	51	44					•					•	•						•		
6m(8m) seven f	51	39	•						•				•							•	
6m(9f) eight m	51	33	•							•						•				•	
7f(1m) eight m	44	87			•		•										•			•	
7f(2f) nine f	44	80		•					•								•	•	•		
7f(3m) one m	44	72		•				•									•		•		
7f(4f) two f	44	64			•			•											•	•	

Nine Star Ki Number	Adult number page	Child number page	Child number is mother to house it resides in (p.105)	Child number is son to house it resides in (p.106)	Child number is in house that it controls (p.106)	Child number is in house that it is controlled by (p.107)	Child number resides in house of same transformation as itself (p.108)	Adult number supports child number (p.117)	Adult number controls child number (p.117)	Child number supports adult (p.116)	Child number controls adult number (p.118)	Adult and child number are same (p.107)	Adult and child transformation (not number) are same (p.118)	Males Same/same (p.121)	Males Same/opposite (p.121)	Males Opposite/same (p.122)	Males Opposite/opposite (p.122)	Females Same/same (p.121)	Females Same/opposite (p.121)	Females Opposite/same (p.122)	Females Opposite/opposite (p.122)
7 f (5 m/f) three m	44	57				•				•						•	•	•	•		
7 f (6 m) four f	44	51		•							•						•			•		
7 f (7 f) five m/f	44	44	•									•						•	•		
7 f (8 m) six m	44	39	•							•							•		•		
7 f (9 f) seven f	44	33		•					•									•	•		
8 m (1 m) seven f	39	87		•					•					•						•
8 m (2 f) eight m	39	80					•						•		•				•	
8 m (3 m) nine f	39	72	•						•				•							•
8 m (4 f) one m	39	64		•					•					•					•	
8 m (5 m/f) two f	39	57					•					•	•						•	•
8 m (6 m) three m	39	51		•				•					•							•
8 m (7 f) four f	39	44		•				•						•					•	
8 m (8 m) five m/f	39	39					•					•	•							•
8 m (9 f) six m	39	33		•					•					•					•	
9 f (1 m) six m	33	87		•						•						•		•		
9 f (2 f) seven f	33	80	•					•								•	•			
9 f (3 m) eight m	33	72		•						•						•		•		
9 f (4 f) nine f	33	64	•							•							•	•		
9 f (5 m/f) one m	33	57		•				•					•	•			•	•		
9 f (6 m) two f	33	51		•						•				•					•	
9 f (7 f) three m	33	44		•						•							•	•		
9 f (8 m) four f	33	39				•		•					•						•	
9 f (9 f) five m/f	33	33	•									•					•	•		

Part II

♦

THE NINE NUMBERS

♦

In this part, each of the nine numbers has its own chapter. Each chapter comprises a profile, derived from several sources, followed by a narrative.

The sources and implications of data in the profiles is as follows:

Trigram: pictorial representation of the number as conceived of in the I *Ching*

Colour: associated with Transformation Phase as agreed upon in *An Anthology of I Ching* and by Tibetan astrologer Sangye Wangchuk

Element: as conceived in Law of Five Transformations

Internal Representation: from Law of Five Transformations and several volumes on Oriental Medicine

Physiognomy: where the qualities of the Transformation Phase are perceived by others; from *An Anthology of I Ching*

Primary Attribute: based on trigram properties as described in the I Ching. This is a basic character quality.

Family Member Type: based on the I Ching and its interpretation of the interactions of different Transformation Phases as if in a family

Management skills: From the work of Warren Bellows and Nancy Post; how each transformation type best functions and interacts in groups

Occupations: From *An Anthology of I Ching*

Illnesses: From *An Anthology of I Ching* and other sources on Oriental medicine

Development Enhanced By: from *An Anthology of I Ching* and Tibetan Astrologer Sangye Wangchuk

Tincture: a herbal extract that enhances qualities of the transformation phase, as conceived by Rex Lassalle, DO. Herbal extracts, when taken in the proper doses as recommended by a herbalist can be used to deal with stress in a particular transformation or as a way of enhancing a particular transformation strength.

Best Suited With: best relationship possibilities as conceived in *Bai Hwa Zhong-guo Qi Xue Ming Li Ru Men* by Sinda Taguchi (see Chapter 13. Numbers in bold type (**1**) are the most auspicious.

Directions to Travel: from the *Bai Hwa Zhong-guo Qi Xue Ming Li Ru Men* and John Mann and Stephen Gagne's *The Nine Ki Handbook*. Numbers here indicate wherever these numbers are situated on the Magic Square at the time one wants to travel. Numbers in bold type are the most auspicious.

Cautiousness in Travelling: From same sources as Directions to Travel. These are directions one should avoid or be cautious in travelling towards. Numbers in bold type indicate the most inauspicious directions. Note that the number of the profile being examined may be listed here. What this means is that when that number is in the House of Five (i.e. the centre) travel is not recommended at all.

The narratives have the following pattern: General Information, Love Relationships, Business Relationships, Spiritual Matters and General Health Recommendations. This material comprises my own insights blended with the sources referred to in the text and the Bibliography.

A further useful clarification has to do with the subheading in each description, General Health Recommendations.

Generally speaking, if our life and lifestyle is more in line with the dynamics and recommendations listed for the year that we were born in, that is our adult natal year, we maintain relatively good health. When under stress, thus when our month or child natal month number is activated, we may need to pay closer attention to the general health recommendations as found in the month number narrative, especially if we are showing physical or emotional symptoms associated with our month (child natal) number. Once we have followed the recommendations of the month number for some relative time period and our health is returning to 'normal,' one should then return to recommendations indicated in the year or adult natal number material.

Nine

◆ Profile

Number: 9

Trigram: ☲ Li (Clarity, the Fire)

Colour: Maroon (purple)

Element: Fire

Internal representation: Blood system, heart, small intestine, heart governor, triple heater, glandular system

Physiognomy: Eyes

Symbolized by: Pheasant, goldfish, crab, shrimp, oyster, turtle

Primary attribute: Clarity

Family member type: Middle daughter

Management skills: Yin: Priority-Setting – selling priorities, marketing, sorting, problem solving, transforming, discriminating; and The Networker – team-building, socializing, customer relations, setting climates (the atmosphere)

Yang: The Coordinator – directing, controlling, cooperating, defining roles, conducting; and The Communicator – appreciating, internal communications, protecting, committing, creating trust, expressing, promoting

Occupations: Public servant, fundamentalist, writer, artist, artisan, optometrist, war correspondent, armourer, book dealer, beautician, publisher, diplomat, judge, barrister, politician, advertising agent, broker, fortune teller, horticulturist

Illnesses: Brain tumors, mental illnesses, heart ailments, blood disorders, fevers, eye diseases, glandular disorders, upper gastro-intestinal tract complaints

Development enhanced by: Being a light for self and others

Tincture: Nutmeg

Best suited with: 2,**3,4,5**,8

Directions to travel: 2,3,4,5,8 (best **2**)

Cautiousness in travelling: 1,6,7,9

◆ Narrative

Nine is the most expansive of all the Nine Star Ki numbers, being at the beginning of the nine-year cycle as it spirals through time. This expansive quality has more to do with brilliance than all-pervasiveness. Along these lines, fire is associated with gestation in Five Transformation Theory, where what has been born is expanding and begins to be distinguishable in its own right. No longer nascent or a bud, the initial brilliance of potential begins to shine forth.

Nine-fire people are the embodiment of brilliance. They are generally passionate, radiant in appearance and charged in their emotional experience and expression. Thus like a star that is seen in the distance, a nine-fire person tends to be noticed. If they walk into a crowded room, they are noticed almost immediately by those present. This is not only in terms of a relatively beautiful or handsome appearance; their word also has a strong impact on others. When grounded, they possess an unmatched clarity and brilliance in perception and expression. Because of this natural charisma in appearance and word, for a nine-fire person to remain balanced and sensitive to their environment, they must be conscious of their impact.

Their words are naturally impressive, even if there is no substance to them. Thus they could 'sell water by the river'.

Inevitably they may mislead people at times. This is not because they consciously wish to deceive. On the contrary, nine-fire people tend to be very blunt and they cannot keep secrets. It is just that when caught in the limelight they get ungrounded and 'flamboyant'. Words can unwittingly slip out. This can make others around them cautious and even mistrusting of them. Being conscious of their appearance, as others around them are, they may have a tendency to draw conclusions on insufficient evidence, from appearances only.

Without fuel to burn, fire cannot exist. Thus, nine-fire people need to feel the support and care of those around them. At the same time, this does not mean they have close friends. Because of their charisma, they have many acquaintances. But friends come and go. Yet they are incredibly trusting of others to the point of being naïve at times.

Loyalty is an issue in their relationships, possibly because it is difficult for them to maintain lasting friendships. The nine-fire person cannot believe that people could have covert or ulterior motives. At times they may be asked or 'put up' to be the spokesperson for groups or causes. They are excellent in this role and will usually succeed in putting the point across. However, if challenged directly, the nine-fire person may retreat, looking for support from the crowd – only to find that no one is there. Even so, this person is very forgiving. The idea of bearing a grudge is a preposterous notion to them.

Life generally moves rather easily for a nine-fire person and because this is so for them, they assume that it is the same for others. Thus their expectation of others may be unrealistic. (They can also give an impression of having everything under control and thus find that when they are in need, no one really is there to help because no one can believe that there could be a problem for them.) As life usually goes the way they want it to, they may live under the assumption that that is how it should be. If it doesn't there must be a problem 'out there'.

Nine-fires are not particularly competitive. They assume that they should win. While they hate to lose, the feeling of loss soon disappears as they move on to the next thing. Their natural tendency is to feel joyful and light-hearted about life. If placed under stress, or if this transformation is that of their natal month, the predominant negative emotional response will be one of anxiety. Because of their light-hearted quality and sense that life should move easily, when they experience the contrary or see the hardships of others, they will often express a genuine sadness.

Love Relationships

Nine-fires are romantic by nature and express emotion quite easily. These traits plus their attractiveness makes them a flame around which many moths will gather. They are rarely without a partner but, at the same time, have to deal with the fact that they will naturally attract all sorts of people without initiating anything in particular. Thus they can be considered arrogant, fickle and teases. They may actually be dumbfounded by such accusations, as their naturally naïve character often makes them unconscious of their impact.

As a flame needs fuel to burn, so nine-fire people look to relationships with those more stable than themselves. The I Ching image for fire is expressed by the word 'clinging'. Thus nine-fire people may find themselves overly attached to those to whom they feel attracted. They can abandon themselves to a relationship, whether it be of short or long duration, and during that relationship they will be absolutely faithful – and expect the same from their partners. They may have fantasies of affairs, but that is usually as far as it goes. Although somewhat clinging, when a relationship is over for them, it's over. They will be sad, possibly anxious about what will happen next. But sooner or later another person will come along.

Although fire is considered a masculine notion in many systems of thought, Oriental systems classify it as female (yin) and the flaming expansive quality of this transformation phase makes a nine easier for women to handle as a natal year than for men. (This, however, may just be cultural, as physical and emotional expressiveness and passion are more 'acceptable' in women, as is the tendency to speak and act on feeling or intuition.)

Business Relationships

A nine-fire person is a natural in positions of leadership, communication and selling. Leadership for a nine implies being a figurehead rather than a mastermind. Although not creative *per se*, they can create excitement around ideas and situations, and can act as catalysts. Their clarity and directness can also be quite disarming and useful in sorting out situations that are muddled in some way.

Because of their charisma and natural tendency to be in the lead, a nine-fire person may feel that anything they do is all right, and they therefore may have a tendency to jump the gun. Pointed in the desired direction, they will promote an idea or product successfully. They are excellent at making and developing contacts in a community or organization, and are therefore good at public relations. And within an organization, their passionate nature may express itself as a zeal that is very morale-building. They can value the team and appreciate relationships that make things work. At the same time, this does not mean that such a person would do well in a personnel position. To get involved on a deep level with fellow workers may have rewards for them on a personal basis, but in a professional setting it can be stultifying to the nine-fire's natural abilities. They are much better at bringing out and using the skills of others than dealing with personalities in the work environment.

They are only average in their financial abilities, and are not inclined to save. Their expenses therefore often match their incomes. Thus although adept at surviving, a nine-fire person is not someone an organization is advised to put in a position where conservation and development of finances is needed.

Spiritual Matters

As fire lights up the dark, revealing what is present, so nine-fires have the potential for strong discriminating awareness. Their gift is being able to distinguish what is and is not meaningful. Rooted in earth and reaching towards heaven, they have a very direct approach to spiritual matters. Even the most profound or esoteric truths may be just obvious facts for them.

Thus nine-fires can be a light for themselves and those around them. What they need to guard against is being caught up in their emotions. They should attempt to temper their tendency to get caught up in mere appearances and allow their mind to settle upon what they are perceiving. Thus first impressions and a keen intuition can be backed by intellectual clarity.

General Health Recommendations

Nine-fires should guard against over-indulgence in various aspects of life. Under stress, especially if the nine-fire is the natal month, the natural joy that they exude may be transformed into an anxiety that overshadows them. This can have an adverse effect on the functioning of their upper gastro-intestinal tract, heart and glandular system. The yin-style personality expression of this would be slow laboured action and speech. The yang-style expression of anxiety would be the hysterical, constantly jabbering, nervously laughing personality.

A well-rounded vegetarian diet is recommended as saturated fats found in animal foods may contribute to heart and circulatory problems. Some white meats such as fish and poultry may be acceptable. Nine-fires would also do best to avoid hot spices. Stimulants such as coffee and alcohol are best avoided as they may weaken and irritate the upper gastro-intestinal tract.

Exercise should emphasize gentle, flowing motion. Tai Chi would be excellent, as would forms of exercise that involve stretching and joint movement. Joint movements especially enhance movement of blood and its reoxygenation.

Eight

◆ Profile

Number: 8

Trigram: ☶ Ken (Keeping Still, the Mountain)

Colour: White

Element: Earth

Internal representation: Back, spleen, pancreas, stomach

Physiognomy: Hands

Symbolized by: Dog, bull, ox, leopard, mouse

Primary attribute: Keeping Still

Family member type: Youngest Son

Management skills: The Producer – distributing, nurturing, transporting, supporting, maintaining, delivering, producing, integrating, attention to detail

Occupations: Monk or nun, clergy, sculptor, service worker, police or civil service, bank teller, educator, beautician

Illnesses: Arthritis, fatigue, nasal difficulties, leg disorders, constipation, deep muscular pains, blood sugar imbalances, depression, feelings of hopelessness

Development enhanced by: Introspection and developing inner perception

Tincture: Cardamon

Best suited with: **9**,6,7

Directions to travel: 2,6,7,9, (best **2**)

Cautiousness in travelling: 1,3,4

◆ Narrative

This is the most yang of the earth element numbers and as such is ascribed such attributes as heaviness and stability, like a mountain. It represents the greatest solidification of matter in the maturation phase of Fire Transformation Theory. An eight-earth person accomplishes what they want through slow and persistent singleness of direction. The slow and methodical way in which they go about doing things can drive others to distraction. It can even seem that nothing is being accomplished. This is due to the fact that their action is deepening rather than spreading; they delve down into whatever it is that they are wanting to pursue. As a result their accomplishments are usually well founded.

At the same time, their meticulous attention to detail can foster a myopic tendency which leads them to get lost in detail, resulting in feelings of confusion and not being able to prioritize. Thus, while in moments of strength they seem confident, strong-willed, single-minded and perhaps even egotistical, there is a tendency to be indecisive, fragile, perhaps even timid at times of stress. When lost in the detail and depths of their investigation, they may act utterly helpless and need bolstering and stimulation from those around them in order to get their feet back on the ground.

An aspect of their single-minded focus is that they are loyal to others, to causes, or to whatever they see as significant in their lives. When balanced, this loyalty can create a tenacity which others may be shocked to see, as such people often appear calm and steady. Eight-earths are the most stubborn of the numbers and may even manifest extreme competitiveness when challenged. Such traits may also work against them if their loyalty leads them to abandon their better judgement and become involved in situations which they have not properly investigated. There is a tendency towards fanaticism.

An eight-earth is hard to read emotionally. In moments of elation or depression, their appearance can seem rather unchanged. They also conceal their strengths and weaknesses. Because of this unaffected surface, others often view eight-earth people as steady and reliable. Thus they often find themselves to be in the role of counsellor to others. They are naturally caring people who will go deeply into whatever it is others tell them. They must, therefore, develop detachment, otherwise they may find themselves involved more deeply in matters than is useful for them or the person who has come to them. They have a tendency to get over-involved and thus to worry about people and situations. This is especially true under stress.

Changes happen slowly on a mountain. Thus when it comes to decisions in their own lives, or in interactions with others, timing is something eight-earths need to address, as they have a tendency to be hesitant to the point of distraction. Generally they do not adapt well to changes they have not initiated themselves. This is not due to arrogance *per se*, but their manner of slow deliberation can lead others to conclude that the eight-earth is 'stuffy' or conservative.

Love Relationships

As eight-earth people tend to treat all experiences as deep issues, so it is with their emotional and physical expression. In terms of sexuality, eights have a very strong and enduring sex drive, although they may not be overt in expressing it. Thus others may too quickly judge them as sexless or passionless, whereas in fact their sex drive is just very slow to rise and is something which they tend to keep private. Despite all their outer appearance of stoicism, the eight-earth is a sensitive person deep down, who can be hurt by the lack of understanding others may have of how they operate in such matters.

A partner needs to be aware of the eight-earth person's sensitivity and reserve in matters of sexuality. If badgered too much, they will either not respond at all or display some outer affection of emotion out of a sense of duty rather than true feeling.

Once aroused, eight-earth people are single-minded. Once they find someone who stirs their interest, they will tirelessly pursue them. They do not 'shop around'. Yet they are not moralistic. It is as if in the interest of emotional economy they stick to those to whom they feel attracted. Thus they usually combine love and marriage well and enjoy establishing a home with all its daily affairs and routines. Women of this number enjoy the security of home life, but may worry excessively about mundane matters. Men will see themselves as providers and protectors. However, they can also be chauvinistic, especially in the way they show disdain for women who do not interest them or meet their expectations. In such situations, an eight-earth man may be a gossip.

Business Relationships

Generally eight-earth people are level-headed in business matters. They are not innovative, but once given an idea to pursue, they will work on the details intensely and create products of superior quality. They are usually diligent and demonstrate a pragmatic loyalty in working situations. They like to be acknowledged for what they do and feel slighted if their efforts go unnoticed. This does not mean, however, that they want to be put in the spotlight.

The eight-earth person is good as a distributor of information, goods, funds, etc. They can bring things together and keep movement going in a desired direction. They know what it takes to keep a staff team moving on a task. It is much better to keep them focused on tasks rather than personnel concerns, as they have a tendency to get over-involved in the lives of others. Under stress, they may exhibit an unhealthy co-dependency. It is advisable for eight-earth people to learn how to set boundaries.

As regards their personal finances, they are usually successful. They know how to get the most out of limited resources. This may be noticed particularly in younger people, and they get better at it over time. However, they are not ones to question closely about their financial affairs. They like to invest (especially in property), and may keep several bank accounts so that other people cannot work out their financial worth. In a business setting, they will be an asset, so long as they are told where to put money. If they are made a primary financial adviser or put in the position of directing where the money is to go they may make wild speculations or hold out until the 'big one' – whatever the 'big one' is conceived to be – comes along.

Spiritual Matters

The eight earth person's natural tendency towards stillness and constancy finds its highest expression in the creation of a peaceful yet deep spiritual life. These people need to work on understanding the workings and nature of the world around them – the process rather than the minute details. They will find such spiritual contemplations easier in a clean, orderly environment. A shrine or altar which shows respect for earthly forces and elements is helpful for them. Such contemplations can ease their tendency towards making everything solid in their lives, including a notion of themselves, thus lightening their load. Spiritual life needn't be serious, intense and heavy – just well considered.

General Health Recommendations

Because of their natural density (regardless of physical appearances) eight-earth people should avoid foods and lifestyles that create lethargy or may over-activate pancreatic functions. There is a natural tendency towards hypoglycaemia or diabetes, especially if this is the natal month number transformation, or if the person is placed under much stress. The psychological expression of this tendency is continual worry, depression, self-doubt and hopelessness. Foods that exacerbate the physiological and psychological tendencies are sugar, alcohol, cakes and pies. A diet of grains, beans, vegetables, fruits and some animal food is recommended. The emphasis in vegetables should be on mineral-rich sea vegetables in small quantities daily and on green leafy vegetables. Winter squash in season is also excellent.

Eight-earth people should do exercises that involve loosening, stretching and the movement of lymph. If their occupation involves sitting for considerable periods of time, they should pay particular attention to posture and take breaks where they can stretch and loosen their hips and neck muscles. Lighting in their work space should be full-spectrum and natural. Periodic Swedish-style or Tragering (lymphatic-type) massage is recommended.

Seven

◆ Profile

Number: 7

Trigram: ☱ Tui (Joyousness, the Lake)

Colour: Red

Element: Metal

Internal representation: Speech organs, lungs, large intestine, skin

Physiognomy: Mouth (lips)

Symbolized by: Sheep, birds, deer, elk, simians

Primary attribute: Joyousness (sense of ease)

Family member type: Youngest Daughter

Management skills: The Evaluator – performance evaluation, accounting, refining, evolving, managing change, comparing, contrasting, controlling quality, developing quality circles, terminating

Occupations: Public relations, entertainment industry, savings and loans worker, banker, publican, lecturer, dentist, food processing and distribution, spokesperson

Illnesses: Chest and breast difficulties, pelvic disorders, hip joint disorders, skull injuries, lung and large intestine imbalances, skin disorders

Development enhanced by: Recognition of spirituality and joy in giving to others

Tincture: Mullein or raspberry

Best suited with: 2,5,8,1

Directions to travel: 6,2,8,1

Cautiousness in travelling: 3,4,7,9

◆ Narrative

The metal or air element is associated with autumn – the time of harvest. It is also a time of changes and reflection.

Seven-metal people do experience a tremendous amount of actual change, especially in the early part of their lives. Along with the changes in their lives comes a keen sensitivity to those changes. They seem to possess an innate appreciation of the texture of life in all its dimensions and phases. Because of this sensitivity, they project an aura of knowing what is going on. Thus others are naturally attracted to them. They are people's people. Others may see the seven-metal person as someone who has everything under control. Some of this may be because of what the seven-metal has actually experienced. But because of the wide range of their experiences, they can draw inferences from and help others in circumstances they may know little or nothing about personally.

Other transformation phase people may go out of their way to look for experiences. But the seven-metal person is an accumulator. Changes and experiences readily come to them. They are not initiators, but harvesters of what the world offers to them. Thus they can develop a sense of entitlement, and others may view them as lazy. From the seven-metal person's point of view, however, they are just waiting for things to happen for them – which they usually do.

Because of the accumulating quality in their nature, the

material world and possessions are usually no problem for these people. They may squander fortunes yet be able to generate funds whenever they need them. They are fond of jewellery. They are meticulous about their appearance; hair and clothes are arranged stylishly. They are keenly aware of aesthetics generally: fine art, decor, and such like. Yet with all this metal-like precision, there is usually one area in their life that is totally chaotic or a mess.

Seven-metal people are naturally reflective. They are excellent speakers and can captivate the people around them with the richness of the language they use. Although eloquent, this does not mean that they know what they are talking about or that what they are saying is true. They are interested more in appropriateness than accuracy. In personal relationships the purpose behind their white lies or approximate truths is not to deceive deliberately or to impress, but rather to avoid rocking the boat. Seven-metal people have a sense of insecurity which often leads them to speak or act in a way that will ensure that others remain their friends or at least are not offended. They abhor arguments and will go to almost any lengths to avoid offence. The advantage of this is that they make brilliant diplomats and can often resolve conflicts between other people or with someone close to them. They are generally 'up-beat' people and their optimism can be infectious. At the same time, this aura of confidence can in times of need put them in a position where the support they need is not forthcoming or is ineffective. They may be the object of other people's envy or jealousy.

While life in all its changes presents challenges to the seven-metal, to some extent they deal with these challenges by maintaining a strong bond with their past and their roots. They are romantic and at times nostalgic. This may operate as a means of buffering themselves from the full impact of events. Their 'work hard, play hard' philosophy of life keeps them in touch with their childlike nature. Thus they are loved by children. Their families are very important to them, yet there are times when their pleasure-seeking ways lead them to be lax in attending to family responsibilities.

In general their relationships with others appear superficial. Their sharp, reflective minds make them aware of life's changes and the concerns that others may take to heart are, for the seven-metal, just signs of the times – something to be lived through.

Thus the seven-metal may have a tendency to discount others' experiences, to gloss over rather than support others in dealing with their own processes.

Love Relationships

Being nostalgic, easy-talking and generally attractive, seven-metal people easily attract partners. When they see someone they are attracted to, they can create situations in which it seems that the other is taking the initiative. They can control events while seemingly appearing as the victim of other people or of circumstances. In some instances this can manifest as passive aggression.

Seven-metals are very sensuous people. Making love must therefore be something like a fine art, where subtlety makes all the difference. Part of this comes from a desire to heighten their own pleasure and embellish their sense of self. But at the same time, they enjoy seeing their partner experience pleasure. Such an attitude usually arises from a sense of how things should be – what their notion of a *quality* relationship or encounter should be. Thus they may have a difficult time adapting to someone else's perception of what quality might be.

They cannot say no and may find themselves in situations which they come to realize are not to their liking. In such circumstances, they may suddenly drop the relationship. This can happen repeatedly, partly because of their personal sense of aesthetics or because the relationship changes for them and the romance is gone. Thus sevens may find themselves going through many encounters and affairs, trying to recapture a feeling.

If they do marry – and many may choose not to – they should take their time selecting a partner. Using their keen senses and evaluative abilities, they should choose a long-term partner in a more mindful rather than sensuous frame of mind. Here, watching one's heart with one's head is good advice.

Business Relationships

These are 'work hard, play hard' people. The seven-metal is not one to take work home. Work is work and home is home. When it's party time, no thought of work exists in the seven-metal's mind.

Seven-metals are not initiators. Nor are they particularly good at completing tasks. However, they are brilliant at evaluating processes, paying attention to quality, and are thus good at setting standards. Within a business venture they are agents of change. However, where others are involved they may appear to be lazy because of their 'wait and see' attitude. This attitude may, however, be an asset in that the seven-metal may be aware of subtle trends and patterns that are building to a maturing of events undetected by others around them. If others become irritated or impatient with this attitude and press too hard, the seven-metal may retreat to an even more distant (passive) position or just leave the situation altogether. As they are resourceful, they are generally confident that there is always someone out there looking for their talents.

Quality control and public relations are natural areas for the seven-metal. If an employee has to be fired or made redundant, their diplomatic ways and likeableness will probably smooth the process over for both sides. They are also excellent at running businesses that emphasize aesthetics, such as restaurants, art galleries or jewellery shops.

Spiritual Matters

The I Ching trigram for the seven-metal is the Joyous Lake (Tui). Like a calm, cool lake it is characterized by a gentle calm exterior and a strong, deep interior.

Seven-metal people can appear calm on the surface and have the capacity to reflect anything that is around them. Because of this surface veneer, the depth of a seven-metal may remain hidden, even to themselves. They have a tendency to become preoccupied with what appears on the surface – like being involved with a mirage. They may even recognize that there is more to what is going on than the surface appearance. Yet because they get caught up in the excitement of the experience as it appears, the deeper meanings of what is going on may elude them.

The more preoccupied they become in this way, the more it is like a lake that becomes turbulent. They then see only distortions and appear quite shallow. They may even be labelled as 'air heads' or as having a 'mind like a sieve'. This trend applies especially to the reactivated seven-metal child or to a seven-metal adult placed under extreme stress. In both cases, they can become 'experience junkies' – going after experiences just for the sake of having them.

Thus seven-metals need to be aware of addictive attitudes and cultivate time and space for quietness. Breathing-style meditations are useful to calm the mind and body. Once the lake is allowed to calm down, the reflection on the surface can then be contemplated and evaluated. Thus seven-metal people, when seeing things clearly, can bring up from their depths awareness and perceptions that may have been hidden from themselves and from others. Although they themselves may not recognize it at first, seven-metal people who give themselves time to drink from their own depths can experience a lasting sense of joy.

Meditation practices that have healing (for themselves and for others) as an emphasis are also recommended.

General Health Recommendations

This element has as its primary organs and tissues the lungs, colon and skin. These three are vital in the mediating of change in our lives. As we change climate, environment or season, the skin acts as an external protective barrier, the colon as an internal one, and the lungs as a way of adjusting to the changes by modifying the respiratory input for the body. The impact on the skin, colon and lungs can be due to the physical changes in themselves, our psychological or emotional response to the changes, or more likely both. The yang emotional imbalance a person may experience when under stress is rigid control; the yin imbalance is totally groundless and not able to get a grip on anything. Both arise out of clinging or attachment which is something the seven-metal person needs to address. The meditation processes recommended in the section on Spiritual Matters are useful for this.

As regards lungs, air quality is important. In addition to breathing exercises such as pranayama from the yoga tradition, air baths as recommended in Shizuko Yamamoto's *Barefoot Shiatsu* are helpful, as is scrubbing the skin with a stiff brush or loofa when bathing: stimulation of the skin benefits the lungs. (By the same token the use of poor-quality cosmetics and petrochemically based colognes and perfumes are injurious to the lungs and colon.) Exercises which encourage an evenness of breath such as Tai Chi and various martial arts are preferred to aerobic exercise where over-stimulation and forced or chaotic breathing may 'blow' the person out in the long run.

The quality of foods should be considered for lung, colon and skin health. Mucus-forming foods should be reduced or eliminated. Little or no dairy produce should be taken – depending of course on climatic considerations and personal constitution. Raw fruit should be reduced and replaced with cooked fruit. Moreover fruit mixtures such as fruit salad could prove detrimental.

More specifically for colon health, besides the above considerations, a diet rich in fibre is advised. Meats should be reduced and used as a complementary rather than a primary food. Old food that may have on its surface a high concentration of candida microbes and food that has lost its vitality due to refrigeration or freezing should be kept to a minimum. Care should be taken not to change the diet radically, too quickly or too often, as this will upset the intestinal flora and may lead to the rapid onset of disease.

Although all the recommendations made here are prudent for virtually every one of us, they are of especial importance to those who have a metal transformation phase as one of their natal influences.

Finally, seven-metals need to be sure to maintain some routine that provides them with enough stimulation to help in adapting to change. There may be a tendency to be either very lazy or excessive, and such tendencies need to be seen clearly for what they are.

Six

◆ Profile

Number: 6

Trigram: ☰ Ch'ien (Heaven, the Creative)

Colour: White

Element: Metal

Internal representation: Mind (pineal gland), lungs, large intestine, skin

Physiognomy: Skull, head

Symbolized by: Tiger, horse, lion

Primary attribute: Creative

Family member type: Father

Management skills: The Inspirer – equilibrating, inspiring, resonating, setting standards on ethics and task specification, balancing, receiving, moral leadership

Occupations: President, chairman, dictator, military commander, prime minister, king, government service, industrial machinery, lawyer, jeweller, salesman, priest, teacher, sports equipment salesman, psychiatrist, counsellor, campaigner, manager of transport-type venture

Illnesses: Lung ailments, swellings, migraines, skin disorders (acne), broken bones, heart ailments

Development enhanced by: Experience of oneness (universal brotherhood), working towards this

Tincture: Cubeb

Best suited with: 2,5,8,1

Directions to travel: 2,8,7,1

Cautiousness in travelling: 3,4,6,9

◆ Narrative

This is the most yang of numbers according to the I Ching interpretation. Six-metal manifests full creative energy and thus six-metal people tend to be activators, people who accomplish things in all facets of their lives. The creative energy that they exude is not that of an innovator. Rather, they can take ideas from others and bring them into being.

Six-metal is also considered the primal father number. Consequently people of this number feel a tremendous sense of duty and responsibility. At an early age they demonstrate this in their family. They are often the child that watches over and takes care of their siblings. If they are younger and not made directly responsible for them in some way, the six-metal may spend time worrying about them. If a parent is missing from the family, six-metal children will often rise to the task of taking on the roles and responsibilities of the missing adult. Such care and concern can also extend to others in their lives. In fact, these are very moral and socially oriented people. They experience the world as having or needing order. This can make six-metals over-involved and somewhat tense – coiled for action. They find it difficult to unwind or relax, unlike seven-metals. They have strong views and strong ideals and are quite willing to argue to get their point across, even if it involves going to excessive lengths to rationalize their position, views and actions. They do not take criticism well and may, especially under stress, exhibit a tendency to see the world in good/bad, black/white terms.

Six-metal people are very aware of their own weaknesses, but conceal them well out of fear of being exploited by others. On the other hand, this means that they can be overly self-critical and as a result sabotage their own efforts. They can then lapse into lethargy, blaming themselves for their predicament. In more extreme cases, they can become paralyzed by an overwhelming sense of guilt. However, such periods are relatively short in duration, and the six-metal then musters energy for the next conquest.

This self-critical attitude can be projected outward by six-metals, in which case they can be quite cutting towards others, expressing high expectations and being rather undiplomatic if they do not live up to their expectations or standards. Thus, six-metals must be aware of their power and influence over other people. If properly directed, the six-metal can become a shining example to others, with the capacity to encourage people towards heights they themselves may not have imagined they could attain.

The past plays a very important part in the lives of six-metal people. They try to keep lessons from the past in perspective while they build the present and plan for the future. At the same time, they are not the sort of people who reveal all their plans: they need to know that what is produced will have the marks of their authorship.

Six-metals work very hard and are achievement-oriented. Their motives may be either highly egotistical or highly altruistic. In either case, they accumulate power, wealth and status rather easily. In the process of acquiring such things, they may use those around them and thus may find themselves as social outcasts. However, if they focus their intentions on ideals that benefit others, they can be quite magnanimous. Their sense of caring and command over the world around them can lead them to be leaders in almost any field they choose. It all depends on their ideals and perspective. They can be great educators, company chairmen, religious leaders or tyrants. Their ability to command is natural and thus often carries with it an air of nobility and elegance. How these traits express themselves will be determined by the society or circle in which they find themselves.

Love Relationships

Although the material and physical world is easy for the six-metal person to master, mastering their own emotional states in relationships is another matter. As family and social mores play a central role in their identity, being in a properly defined relationship is important to them. Along with this comes a very strong sex drive; the sex act itself is viewed in the light of morality and social order. Thus a six-metal person will tend to have strict definitions as to what is appropriate and not appropriate in a relationship and in sex: timing, place, act, and so forth. This means that there can be an over-emphasis on performance, with a resulting loss of spontaneity. If they are rigid in their views, they may seem over-confident, nonchalant, perhaps cavalier.

When under stress, men of this number (especially if it is their natal month number) may be either domineering or chauvinistic, or else may dominate the females in their lives by acting as though they were weak and needy. Not wishing to appear as failures, they may go to excessive lengths to perform duties and tasks which their partner requests or demands of them. They are also gullible and easily succumb to flattery. A woman of this number may be compelled to take on more family responsibilities than she is truly capable of handling, thus feeling over-burdened yet obliged to perform in that way.

Basically, a six-metal person seeks a deep and true relationship. And this does help them to feel that they have a proper place in the world. If this is achieved, then a six-metal becomes a devoted and awesome lover, provider or homemaker and family person.

Business Relationships

As I have said, this person is not an innovator but an activator. Because they like to be part of or in charge of the established order, six-metal people do not look for ideas of change. But they do get things done.

Within a corporate setting, the six-metal person is difficult to give orders to. At the same time, they do not make the best of managers. If they can act on their own within a supportive setting, they can be an inspiration to others, providing they do not let success go to their heads. While they are strong-headed, they do not do well if they work in isolation or solitude. The stimulation from the outside provides the oil for their machinery to function.

Six-metals think big in financial terms. Value for money is something they understand well. Thus they are good at establishing compensation systems. Women of this number usually acquire wealth quite easily. Men of this number do well, providing they act under their own steam. Both men and women of this number handle money well, but there is a tendency to be tight-fisted. This does not mean that they are conservative; rather, they are accumulators. Generosity usually arises within them when they have a sense that they are benefiting the social order, the company or the community. And they like others around them to know that it is they who have been generous.

They are natural leaders – leaders in their field, leaders of others. No one is better at establishing order than a six-metal person. They do this especially well when it comes to setting standards in ethics and task specification, like a ship's captain getting his ship on course. In such situations, the six's natural brilliance shines forth. If placed under stress (or when the six is the natal month aspect), or where there is more disorder than anticipated, the commanding six may become excessively domineering, and this may in some cases turn into tyranny.

Spiritual Matters

Six-metals have strong psychic abilities and intuitive awareness. Coupled with this is a strong sense of morality and a need to be connected to society, the social structure and community mores. If dietary and lifestyle factors lead them to have an imbalanced yin condition, there may be an over-emphasis on psychic abilities. As the person becomes more ethereally oriented, focusing their attention on invisible or more subtle dimensions of reality, they become ungrounded and lose their practical sensibility and connection to the world around them. If factors make them more yang or tight, they may ignore their intuitive sensitivity and plunge into ardent dogmatism. It is only the balance between these two facets, and a lifestyle that supports it, which leads them deeper into their spiritual life. Six-metals are generally the most traditionally religious of the numbers. Balancing their intuition with their connection with society, the deeper intuitive knowledge that arises for them can become a wellspring from which they work in society towards peace and universal brotherhood.

Six-metals should make a point of acknowledging the importance of their environment and their ancestry. This serves as an inner and outer protection in their spiritual growth and expression.

General Health Recommendations

These are people of strong constitution. They seldom become physically sick. However, as a result of their tendency towards pride, six-metals may push themselves to their limits too often. This can be the cause of a rapid onset of illness which is difficult to cure. Thus they should be wary of over-exertion and try to cultivate moderation in activities.

Like seven-metals, the health of their lungs, colon and skin is essential for their well-being. Six-metals may exhibit skin problems more than most and should be wary of suppressing symptoms as a solution when changes in diet and lifestyle are needed.

Mental tension and worry can play a major role in the sabotage of a six-metal's health. Thus they need to cultivate relaxation. Breathing exercises combined with observation of postural alignment are useful. Meditative processes that can be practised in a group will probably be more successful than solitary attempts at home. Yoga postures or exercise processes which turn the body upside down can also be useful in providing rich blood and oxygen to areas of the body that may be stagnant from tension and lack of activity. The health measures mentioned in the seven-metal chapter should also be considered.

Six-metals, more than most people, do not like to live within limits that they have not created themselves. Thus they must align themselves with whatever changes they need to make in order for such changes to be truly effective.

Five

◆ Profile

Number: 5

Trigram: ⚏ Female trigram K'un (the Receptive) and ⚎ Male trigram Ken (the Mountain)

Colour: Yellow

Element: Earth

Internal representation: Stomach, spleen, pancreas, lymphatics

Physiognomy: Hands and abdomen

Symbolized by: None

Primary attribute: Catalyst

Family member type: None

Management skills: The Consolidator — catalysing, leading, sorting, critiquing

Occupations: Politician, leader of enterprises, military or police officer, refuse collector, pawnshop owner, secondhand dealer, unskilled labourer

Illnesses: Have to do with excesses, infectious diseases, diarrhoea, circulatory problems, tumours, fever, immune-related diseases, blood sugar imbalances, depression, delusions, high blood pressure, heart disease, possibly gall bladder imbalances

Development enhanced by: Contemplation, listening

Tincture: Rosecan

Best suited with: 9,6,7

Directions to travel: 9,2,6,7

Cautiousness in travelling: 1,3,4

◆ Narrative

Five-earth is the centre of the Magic Square. During a five-earth year, all the transformation phase energies are within their own houses. It is a time of great energy which demands intense reflection. It can also be a time when one feels very much on one's own.

Such characteristics are part of the five-earth person's nature. They are usually quite energetic. They share aspects with both the two-earth and the eight-earth, being caring individuals who have good insight. However, they can be a bit wishy-washy in their expression, becoming indecisive and thus unable to act on their insight. Put in the context of the maturation phase of the Five Transformations, five represents a point at which things are at their most dynamic in the maturation process, where the outer shell of appearance begins to fill in with substances for the first time.

Being in the centre of the Magic Square, the five-earth is like the hub in the centre of the spokes of a turning wheel. At the centre, they can act as a catalyst in the lives of others. They can be extraordinary problem-solvers and often find themselves as leaders, whether it be of a small group, a gang, an army, a nation or a religious order. They can weave order from disarray or come up with solutions for problems within groups. At the same time, a five-earth person can be a very needy individual. They often cannot use their talents to their own advantage. Being in the middle (or the leader), others may expect a five-earth to be more grounded, but in fact, such individuals generally feel as if the ground is moving under their feet constantly. Thus they have a strong longing to find a place or niche for themselves.

Being charismatic and often drawing attention to themselves unintentionally, they are often accused of being egocentric. This is not helped by the fact that the five-earth is rather blunt and stubborn, tends to be impatient, may complain a lot, and has a not-so-helpful tendency to mimic others. In moments of insecurity such traits may become more exaggerated as over-confidence and arrogance. At the root of their insecurity is self-doubt. In times of such self-doubt the healthy scepticism that a five-earth displays in order not to be taken in by others may turn into an unappealing cynicism which can make anyone or anything its target.

The five-earth is a complex personality – someone to be reckoned with. They find few close friends, but can cultivate enemies of greater or lesser intensity rather quickly. Though others may not be able to make sense of their actions and words, the balanced five-earth can be profoundly altruistic and have a deep compassionate heart – traits which will often go unnoticed by those around them.

A five-earth person's life is never uneventful. These people can either have exceptionally good fortune or experience a constant stream of disasters. In times of good fortune, they may become lackadaisical and as a result lose or spend it. If, on the other hand, circumstances are hard for them, they can be quite stoical and bear things that others would find difficult to endure. In such hardship, one will find a five-earth striving against the odds. Their desire for success is very strong. Their means to accomplish their ends are usually innovative. When out of balance this may manifest as impracticality. Having a strong sense that they are somehow on their own in the world, they do not bear criticism or even positive suggestions very well and will, consequently, learn from the 'school of hard knocks'.

As five is in the middle of the nine-year cycle, the expansive yin and contractive yang qualities are somewhat equal. Five-earth people therefore bear both male and female characteristics. This can manifest itself physically as an almost androgynous quality; the men of this number can be rather elegant if not beautiful while the women appear handsome. Within the personality there also exists almost a balance of traits that are classified as 'feminine' and 'masculine'. This can create an inner tension within the five-earth person. They may at times exhibit the keen observation yet superficial ways of the two-earth, while at others manifesting the penetrating insight and attention to detail of the eight-earth person. It all depends on circumstances. Extreme expressions of personality may also create confusion and tension for those around the five-earth person. Such versatility can, however, be an asset in that they are capable of handling diversity in a way that would leave others reeling. Consequently, five-earths tend to be quite unusual people with very interesting lives, people who are often the subject of other people's conversations.

Love Relationships

There is a natural charisma that a five-earth person carries, leading them to find a partner easily. Both males and females of this number can be sexually irresistible to those around them. As regards sex itself, five-earths are the most physically focused of all the numbers. They love to make love, but equally love to see the pleasure they bring to their partners. Because they embrace extremes, partners may find that, at different times, they can either need to receive touch or stimulation or demand to be very physical with their partners. Unless they can maintain a balance within themselves, the intensity they exude coupled with their need or their imposing ways may lead partners to break off relations with them.

For a five-earth, 'variety is the spice of life', and they therefore have tendencies towards infidelity. This does not mean that they do not care for their partners or are fickle. In fact, they can feel within themselves deeply committed to one partner while they have various affairs on the side. Females of this number do this more out of a desire for more contact and more experiences; thus they often find themselves in 'love-triangle' difficulties. The men will be unfaithful to see if they are still attractive to others. Thus five-earth people are not particularly good at homemaking and usually find ways to recruit others to take on domestic responsibilities.

If a partner can tolerate their extremes in moods, needs and tendencies (usually towards infidelity), they will find a five-earth person passionate, caring and deeply committed. If they cannot and choose to leave, the five-earth will be truly saddened. But it won't be long before another person comes into their life.

Business Relationships

The five-earth person could not be classified as the average worker. Some are so motivated that they rise to the top of their profession – and they are good at almost any profession they turn their minds to. Such people are extremely innovative and are excellent synthesizers of what to others would be discordant information. On the other hand, there are those five-earth people who are extremely lackadaisical or channel their more positive tendencies into destructive habits. Thus they can be the best or the worst at anything, depending on their motivation and the situations that circumstances offer them. The extremes that may be noted in different five-earth individuals may also be present in the same individual at different times. The high-flying five may have areas in their life that are not working at all. And it may even be that there are times when they are absolutely brilliant or absolutely helpless at the same task.

In terms of organizational skills, five-earths can seem to be rebellious. One can view them as 'problem' employees or choose to recognize their leadership and catalyzing abilities. While they are not particularly good at completing tasks, getting a five-earth person to spearhead a task force or to act as a spokesman for a project puts them in a position where their charisma and creative energies can come to the forefront. They will also exhibit caring and sharing qualities that can promote harmony within a group, with business partners or with new clients (whom they are good at impressing).

Five-earths have an unusual way of relating to money. While caring and generous to others in many ways, when it comes to money they can be misers. They hold on to their money tightly. As employees, these are people that may query their pay several times, asking where each pound has gone. More than others, they may communicate that somehow they have either been paid the wrong amount or that they should have more. Such attention to finances may lead an employer to view the five-earth as an excellent candidate to handle company money matters. However, where any corporate speculation is involved, employers should be warned that the five-earth, while never personally experiencing any grave financial hardship from which they cannot recover if they so choose, is not so fortunate with the money of others. When it comes to gambling or any financial speculation, five-earths will usually lose more than they gain.

Spiritual Matters

Tibetan tradition views the five-earth person as religious by nature. There is a strong link between them and their ancestors and thus they should make a point of having the veneration of ancestors somehow included in the process of their spiritual life. Fives have very deep longings and needs when it comes to their spiritual life. Yet, because they are quick to think and act, the five-earth person has a tendency to miss the point if it is not obvious. To deepen their understanding, they must therefore practise listening and contemplation. Stillness is needed to balance their restless nature. As five-earths thrive with music around them, the use of bells, drums, ritual music and chanting are useful in nurturing their spiritual development. Such practices can prevent the five-earth from excessive self-involvement and concern.

The five-earth person is naturally altruistic, yet they may find that others dislike them for no apparent reason, other than the fact that they dislike fives just for being themselves. Consequently, they should cultivate the virtues of patience and humility to soften their character.

General Health Recommendations

Five-earth people are generally healthy. If their five is in the adult natal position, they should have a relatively strong immune system and can thus endure adverse environmental conditions and ward off sicknesses that others will be more easily prone to. However, if the five-earth is the child number or if five adults find themselves placed in constantly stressful circumstances, their immunity could drop dramatically.

Five-earth people are prone to illnesses precipitated by going to one extreme or the other. On a physical level, the five-earth person may be very active or extremely inactive. When very active, they may exceed the limits of what their body can endure and may develop heart conditions as a consequence. If continuously underactive or if their over-activity leads them to 'crash', the resultant lethargy may lead to exhaustion and physically related depression.

On an emotional level, if their natural altruism lapses into a co-dependency marked by insecurity and constant preoccupation and worry, the five-earth may become hypercritical and negative (which could also be a source of ulcers). The more self-absorbed or withdrawn from the world a five becomes, the more likely they are to become so lackadaisical that they lose the initiative to respond to life's demands. Thus they may become increasingly doubtful of their own judgement, lapsing into self-denigration and periods of depression.

Such physical and emotional tendencies, coupled with a diet high in stimulants, sugar and additives, as well as prescription and non-prescription mood-altering substances, may result in the diseases I have mentioned as well as hypoglycaemia, diabetes and chemical dependency.

Moderation and balance are keys to a five-earth's continued health and well-being. A diet with few, if any, of the substances mentioned above is recommended. Moderate and above-average levels of exercise are recommended, especially those forms which activate the lymphatic system. Lengthy periods of sitting should be avoided. General Swedish-style massage is recommended periodically. Sleep and times for quality relaxation should be daily routines.

The challenge for a five-earth person is to realize that they possess the greatest of extremes on all levels of their being compared to other people. They have tremendous potential which if nurtured can create a life which is both rewarding for them and nurturing for others.

Four

◆ Profile

Number: 4

Trigram: ☴ Sun (Wind, the Gentle/Penetrating)

Colour: Green

Element: Tree

Internal representation: Nervous system, breathing system (diaphragmatic muscles), gall bladder

Physiognomy: Legs (noticeable eyes – hypnotic)

Symbolized by: Cock, chicken, crane, snake, earthworm, unicorn

Primary attribute: Penetration

Family member type: Eldest Daughter

Management skills: The Decision-Maker – making decisions, individuating, clarifying, scheduling, initiating conflict, structuring, timekeeping

Occupations: Removals industry, shipping, building, furniture construction, advertising, travel agent, business person, mediator, guide, communications industry, teacher, public relations, master of ceremonies, manufacture and/or selling of wood and/or rope and associated products

Illnesses: Colds, hyperactivity, intestinal upsets, gall bladder ailments, connective tissue problems

Development enhanced by: Reflection, concentration, penetration

Tincture: Goldenseal

Best suited with: 1,9

Directions to travel: 9,1,3

Cautiousness in travelling: 2,4,6,7,8

♦ Narrative

Four-tree is the yin or more expansive of the two numbers representing the tree transformation. The tree transformation is also referred to as the space transformation. Both names represent aspects of qualities that both four- and three-tree people exhibit. (For brevity's sake, we shall just refer to the transformation as 'tree'.)

The tree element is symbolic of spring, where fine young shoots break through the ground in an attempt to assert themselves in their environment. There is a sense of freshness, uncertainty and vulnerability in the air that can manifest as an irritable quality.

Four-tree people demonstrate these spring-like qualities. Like young shoots struggling to survive, they want to make it, to be someone. They are independent and determined. However, their determination, which is often expressed by a veneer of toughness, conceals a soft, vulnerable interior. Four-trees are truly ground-breakers: discovering, coming up with new ideas, seeing things as if for the first time. There can be a sense of innocence and wonderment with such people that is reflected in their eyes. In fact, interaction with the world for a four-tree focuses around vision and being able to see things clearly. It is important for a four-tree to make eye contact in order to feel that they are communicating with others. However, their gaze can be quite mesmerizing, as their eyes are deep and hauntingly intense. (Others may find such a gaze intimidating, and may even think that the four-tree is acting as a tempter or temptress. However, there is usually nothing special behind the four-tree's gaze that would bespeak treachery. Of course, such a person usually discovers early on the power of their gaze and will use it to be convincing or to get their own way.)

Although four-trees can see situations in a clear way and possess a high degree of common sense, this does not mean that they necessarily have vast experience or a deep knowledge to back up their perceptions. They are excellent generalists who easily pick up a lot of information just on first impression, as if they had a sixth sense for general tones and feelings. But, because of this impressionability, they may overlook the details or inner workings of circumstances – especially when the circumstances are not quite as straightforward as they seem. Thus fours can become confused by complexities and may project on to such situations all sorts of notions which have little to do with their original perceptions. They may confound their own common sense. And, because they possess a sense of natural maturity of being, others are often convinced by whatever the four-tree says. The four-tree may even know that what they are imparting to others is not exactly right, but it is almost as if the ripening of their perceptions – seeing clearly upon reflection – has not caught up with their mouths.

Fortunately, because they are so sensitive to their environment and the people around them, they never push a hard line and therefore usually try to find some delicate way of bringing things around into a more realistic perspective. Too often, however, they don't get a chance to accomplish this because others have already departed before they can overcome their own insecurities and be more straightforward. This hesitancy and 'beating around the bush' style means the four-tree is often misunderstood. They also cannot keep secrets, especially other people's secrets and they are therefore accused, and rightly so, of breaking confidentiality.

Like the elemental quality of space, the four-tree is an open field for impressions to pour on to. They always have many ideas which appear to them mentally as visual images. Yet when it comes to action, they can only handle one idea at a time. Give a four-tree person too much to do and they will panic or constantly chop and change so that nothing gets done. The more complex the situation, the more likely it is that they will lose their natural perspective and hence their sense of priorities. In fact, priorities for a four-tree are not necessarily determined by what is needed or a desired outcome. Rather, priorities emerge from an intuitive compassion and a sense of the right timing of events.

Timing is very important to the four-tree person. They are, in fact, the most time conscious of all the numbers. Essentially all things have time frames for them and when dealing with a four-tree it is quite useful to spell things out in time frames. When timing is disrupted the four-tree can become frantic and act in a thoroughly confused and disoriented manner. Also, when placed under stress, four-trees lose their ability to estimate realistic times for plans or events. In such circumstances, they usually put things off to the last moment, and are thus often labelled procrastinators. When this occurs, they can genuinely believe that they have allowed enough time for things to take place. They often cannot see that their abhorrence of detail has slowed up timely decisions and that their hesitation and worry actually creates such a predicament. Thus they find themselves living life at a somewhat hectic, jerky pace. Their lives can be filled with constant ups and downs, but the four-tree's attitude generally remains positive. If an idea, notion or situation comes crashing down, there are dozens of others to take their place.

The tree or space transformation has inherent within it the quality of independence. Like the young shoot that breaks the ground, the four-tree person wants very much to emerge and establish their own identity. Yet, like the young shoot, the four-tree person is highly vulnerable to the environment and conditions need to be right for them to succeed in their efforts. As the young shoot needs sufficient water, quality soil, warmth, sunlight and air, so the four-tree needs support for their efforts towards independence. They need to consider and be mindful of their environment and respect the circumstances and people around them who make it possible for them to succeed.

In times when they are uncertain of their strengths, four-trees may abdicate self-control to an authority that appears to be supportive and stronger and more competent than themselves. They then become blindly obedient. Such obedience, however, is usually conditional. In the safety of such support they can once again come to feel confident of their own abilities, at which point it is not uncommon for the four-tree to be back-biting and a rumour monger towards those whom they previously relied on for support.

Because of this obvious symbiotic relationship with their environment and the people around them, people usually have something to say about the four-tree. Thus they may be the subject of gossip. Being forward-moving, however, four-tree people are not likely to be bothered by this. They delicately move through life always discovering, always striving.

Love Relationships

The four-tree is a strong believer in 'true love'. They are the innocents who have romantic notions about the right person, the right relationship and perfect timing. They are therefore very naïve. Yet this naïvety coupled with their emotional maturity, physical expressiveness and deep alluring eyes makes the four-tree person the object of attraction for others.

Although attractive to many people, the four-tree strives to be selective about whom they become involved with. Because of their natural vulnerability, they are rather guarded about conveying their true feelings. When involved with someone, their strong romantic ideals may lead them to project on to a partner all sorts of attributes that have little or nothing to do with who the partner really is. Gradually they may come to see things as they really are, but not before they and their partners have gone through several misunderstandings.

Four-tree people are looking for a deep relationship. Yet it is not uncommon for them to be attracted to people because of their power or influence, rather than because of their character. In such circumstances, they may only wake up to the fact that it was not the person, but the money or status that attracted them after they have become deeply committed.

Nevertheless, because they are generally loyal people, when a relationship is not working out the four is willing to wait for things to come around and improve. A four needs to put effort into communicating more with their partner to clear up confusions. If they do not and the relationship worsens, the strain may lead the four-tree to become uncharacteristically aggressive and cavalier. They may have several extra-marital relations or affairs which to them are of little significance. For them it is just a matter of waiting until the relationship they are in works out, or else until the 'right' person finally comes along.

This is a challenging area in the four-tree's life.

Business Relationships

These are people who do best when employed by someone else. A four-tree will be loyal and productive for an employer to whom they can look up and by whom they feel supported.

Given an idea to explore, the four-tree can run with it, probably farther than anyone else can take it. They have a keen sense of what will and won't work, although working out exactly *how* is not their forte. If such ideas are just their own creation and are not receiving the support of others, the four-tree may take things in too rash or impetuous a direction. However, in the right supportive environment, where they are being encouraged and valued, four-tree people's intuitions about ideas and situations should be trusted. They are efficient and know how to enhance the efficiency of others.

Four-tree people are generally good at clarifying situations, using their common-sense approach to reduce things to simple units to work with. However, if the situation demands increased complexity or there are a lot of undertones or hidden agendas, one can almost see a fog descend over their eyes; their natural common sense is then clouded in a layer of total bewilderment. When this occurs, the four's vagueness, indecision or inaction is not really a ploy to shirk responsibility. Rather, they are simply overwhelmed. A lightening of their load will once again allow their natural abilities to shine forth. A simple way to by-pass this stress response is for the four-tree to develop decision-making tools, instruments, or processes. Whatever device they come up with will probably be all-encompassing.

As regards relationships within a business, the four is generally likeable and sociable, even though they may be the brunt of much office gossip. Because they have a quality of being able to approach issues with sensitivity, they are quite skilled at resolving conflict within an organization.

It is best not to put too much financial responsibility in the hands of a four adult or four child whose adult natal number cannot hold the four quality in check. (Seven- or six-metal to four-tree is advised.) Fours generally have a tendency to part with money easily, and may be convinced by others to invest unwisely.

Spiritual Matters

The four-tree person needs to balance their generalist tendencies with penetration. From the space quality of their transformation phase, it is as if, hovering in space, they get a good sense of what is going on, but need to linger a bit longer, to relax and allow their vision to deepen beyond first impressions. From the tree quality of their transformation phase, they possess a natural irritability which wants to push ahead to the next thing; thus what is present around them is felt, but somewhat blurred. If their spatial quality is enhanced and they can take the time to gain a proper perspective, their actions are magnetizing and rich. Patience needs to be cultivated. This can be a potent antidote to their tendency to be bored or frustrated.

For such people 'cleanliness is next to godliness' is an important dictum to live by. Four-tree people need to take care of their own cleanliness and the cleanliness of their environment to create a serene atmosphere. A serene atmosphere can create more space and less frenetic churning in their lives. They can then have the proper time and space to penetrate deeper into life's mysteries and thus cultivate an inner strength that can prevent their sensitive, vulnerable nature from being overwhelmed or sidetracked.

It is wise for a four-tree to seek out a teacher that they feel kinship with. Meditations where movement is involved, such as yoga or Tai Chi would be advantageous.

General Health Recommendations

Depending on the nature of the stress in a four-tree's life, the insecurity and vulnerability they manifest when imbalanced can produce either a totally flat effect, lacking energy or a body that is tight and rigid (characterized by clenched teeth, with jaw and mouth disease symptoms, and clenched fists with resulting tendencies towards arthritic processes and connective tissue damage). In either case, the root emotional cause is usually frustration and anger. Other possible ailments are indicated in the profile.

A person with tree/space as one of their numbers needs to maintain a healthy level of physical activity. Forms of exercise that activate the musculature and especially the legs are recommended – jogging, brisk walking, swimming, cycling, and any sport that involves running. Four-trees may also have a tendency towards visual difficulties. Right–left brain exercises and therapeutic light apparatuses (like the Downing 'Lumatron', a light-emitting instrument which facilitates the transmission of the full field of the visible light spectrum to the brain via the eyes) are useful, as well as conventional eye exercises.

As regards diet, a four-tree person may be over-fond of flour, oily foods and dairy products high in saturated fats, such as ice cream and sharper cheeses. These should be kept to a minimum as they aggravate the liver and gall bladder. Foods that are high in sodium or potassium (such as snack foods, nightshade vegetables and tropical fruits) should also be avoided, as they can inhibit (in the case of high sodium) or overstimulate (in the case of high potassium) healthy muscular discharge. Calcium-rich foods such as sea vegetables and dark green leafy vegetables are helpful in the diet. Alcoholic beverages should either not be consumed or kept to a minimum as they may increase the tree/space person's general sense of irritation to a point where violence is possible.

A four-tree should avoid being exposed to easterly winds, especially in spring. During such times the torso and throat should be well covered. Massage processes such as shiatsu and sports massage are helpful, as are isometrics. With a proper healthy balance in diet, exercise and relaxation, four-trees can maintain a strong, active physical life with a mental clarity that can give them a zest for living, learning and just being.

Three

◆ Profile

Number: 3

Trigram: ☳ Chen (Thunder, the Arousing)

Colour: Indigo (jade green)

Element: Tree

Internal representation: Liver, feet, musculature, connective tissue

Physiognomy: Vocal system

Symbolized by: Eagle, dragon, swallow, cicada

Primary attribute: Arousing

Family member type: Eldest Son

Management skills: The Planner – planning, mapping, defining borders, adapting, visualizing, brainstorming, recognizing, organizing, environmental scanning

Occupations: Prince, innovator, inventor, constructor, television industry, munitions, engineer, musician, sportsman, surgeon, teacher, writer, speaker

Illnesses: Ulcers, tumours, liver diseases, foot ailments, disorders of the nervous system, phobias, hysteria, muscular disorders, vision disturbances, throat ailments

Development enhanced by: External and internal growth (maturation)

Tincture: Saffron

Best suited with: 1,9

Directions to travel: 9,1,4

Cautiousness in travelling: 2,3,6,7,8

◆ Narrative

As four-tree is the yin expression of the tree/space transformation, where the shoots of spring are just breaking the ground, so three-tree is the more yang expression where the shoots have established themselves in a way that proclaims that spring is really here.

And so it is that three-tree people are bold, if not brash. They are optimistic and garrulous, which is often interpreted by others as being idealistic and foolish. A three-tree person has a tremendous amount of energy and is generally a self-starter. Their minds are very quick and as a result, they may have a tendency to jump the gun. This may take the form of starting a project too soon or with a zeal that often dwindles as completion draws near. The process of doing is more important than the process of completing. On the other hand, just as there are plants that shoot up and mature quickly, but are so fragile that they wither with the heat of summer, so it is with the three-tree person. Their energy and brashness conceal a very delicate sensitivity. Thus there are moments when the three-tree spontaneously creates something which is precious for the moment, but soon fades. Such efforts may go unnoticed by others, as they may be overwhelmed with the three-tree's overall energetic outpouring and intensity.

Three-tree people are 'ideas' people. They love to brainstorm and can usually come up with totally fresh ways of looking at things. They see things in their minds and may thus have the capacity to be visionary. They are creative but usually create in spontaneous ways, without plans. Some of their projects can therefore be total flops. Yet this doesn't daunt the three as there are plenty more ideas to pursue. Unlike the four-tree who has many ideas but must do things one at a time, the three-tree person also has many ideas but likes to do a lot of things all at once.

To an outsider, the manner in which a three-tree sets to work may seem aimless and inefficient. There may not be any detectable order in which things are done. They may start one project, then stop it to go to another one, going on and on like that. The unbalanced stressed three tree may over-extend this process so that very little is accomplished. On the other hand, if their energy is focused, an outsider may suddenly observe that several tasks are completed all at once.

It helps a three-tree to stay more on target if time frames and priorities are established. Long and complicated tasks are generally frustrating for a three-tree unless approached in a way that gives them a sense of time, priority, *and* the mental space in which to be able to do it. After giving them instructions, it's best to leave them alone to get on with it. However, there will be times when the three-tree just can't seem to pull it together because their mind is filled with too many considerations.

Three-trees are quite likeable, but they can also be overwhelming. Their moods or feelings are easily projected into the space around them, which can be either a delight or absolutely stifling to the people around them, depending on circumstances. In general, there is an intensity about them, whether it be positive or negative. They can be quite rude, or shock people with what they say. This is partly due to the fact that three-trees talk as they think and often formulate their ideas as the environment and the people around them allow. Thus they themselves may not even know exactly what they are thinking at any time, and may be quite contradictory in what they say. It all depends on where they are in the formulation process. They should pause to reflect and respond. Threes tend to be quick talkers who in their efforts to straighten out the messages they have given may inadvertently confuse people more. The three-tree can also have the unfortunate habit of finishing sentences for others as they talk.

As spring reflects growth that has not yet matured, so the three-tree person is constantly on the move. They want to act as if they've got everything under control when it isn't quite true.

They don't like admitting to defeat or shortcomings. They are generally the most vain of all the numbers and are very conscious of their physical presentation. Because of this and because of the fact that their movement is fluid and often sensual, young girls who have a three either in the child or in the adult natal position often find themselves being rigidly controlled by their parents. Mothers may be envious of their alluring physicality. Fathers may be harsh or cruel. Although I have no statistics, many women whom I have interviewed who have a three in their Nine Ki numbers have experienced sexual abuse at an early age.

Three-trees either thirst for or are thrust into independence at an early age. Their success in life's pursuits can be meteoric. Of all the numbers, three-trees learn best and accomplish most from their own efforts. They are ambitious and may push things to the limits. When in balance, they have the ability to know when to stop. However, their aims can be tainted with an egotistical pursuit of pleasure and success that can manipulate or disregard the needs of others. When under stress, three-trees may ignore their environment and disregard feedback from those around them. Thus, as quickly as they have gained success, they could squander it. Three-trees are advised to make efforts to get a handle on and master their talents at an early age, lest they endanger their stability in later years.

Frustration is an emotional tendency a three-tree needs to be aware of. If put under stress, which can happen quite easily as they are so independent and don't like to feel challenged or incompetent in some way, their frustration can launch them into fully fledged anger. They can throw tantrums and are the loudest in vocal expression of all the numbers. However, like distant thunder, there is no real danger when they are this way. They usually cool down of their own accord. If confronted by a stronger adversary, the loud, brash three may become conciliatory. Basically they don't want to be hurt or disfigured.

This also partially helps to account for their tendency to flatter. Sometimes it is to protect themselves; at other times, they can do it just to get their own way. The three-tree may have to deal with fallout from their brazen actions and talk, as others may not be as likely to forgive and forget as they are. Because they are action-oriented and visibly seen to be doing something, they are usually blamed when things go wrong in matters that involve them. Blame is something threes will find hard to escape, even in relation to people that they help.

Love Relationships

The three-tree person wants to be in a relationship in which they can be intensely involved and still maintain their independence. Because of these two factors, they may have many love affairs, but will usually marry at an early age. If they do not marry at an early age, it will be because of their many ambitions. In relating to a three-tree, a partner must be aware that their intensity may be equally expressed in other endeavours, though not necessarily other partners.

Their own physical appearance is very important, as is that of their partner. The men of this number are vain and the women jealous of other women's looks. For a three-tree, physicality and the tactile aspects of sexuality are foremost. Such people can literally feel starved if not touched. At the same time, because of their intensity, a three-tree person may find that their strong passions are difficult to contain and thus may wilfully suppress their sexual and emotional desires. This can have a debilitating effect on a physical and emotional level. The men may become distant and aloof or aggressive, depending on the context. The women may view their lives as dull and there is a tendency towards female reproductive tract problems. Because of their intensity and the internal struggle that it produces, balance within a relationship constantly changes, somewhat dramatically.

On the whole, if allowed to express their free-spirited and playful nature, a three-tree can be a vibrant and exciting partner. And if the other partner can accommodate such dynamism and the space a three often needs within a relationship, they may find underneath all the motion and activity a very sensitive and loving individual.

Business Relationships

If one looks at the list of professions in the profile, one notes that they are occupations for independent thinkers, doers or people in the spotlight. Three-tree people do not make good organization people, unless, of course, the organization is theirs.

If they are in an organization three-trees are best suited to positions where they can brainstorm and are given a free rein to run with their creativity. As three-tree is also classified as a space transformation, one may see that their perceptions come from a panoramic vision of situations which makes them excellent strategists. At the same time, they are probably not the ones to carry out the strategy. To put such plans and authority into the hands of a three is to risk endless sidetracks. They are not economical, and may therefore expend a lot of time and energy in different directions from those originally requested. That is why it is best if they are given time frames and priorities with some designated diversionary tasks in order to satisfy their need to spread out. At the same time, another aspect of their panoramic vision is that they are keenly aware of the work environment. So if there is a need to know what the ambiance of the work space is, their perceptions can be trusted.

If a three person is put in a situation where people of higher or more powerful rank try to use their position or put pressure on them, one of several things is likely to happen: they may throw some form of tantrum; they may look for a direct confrontation, or they may just totally withdraw from the scene, which could include walking out. Their independence is that important.

A three-tree person needs to work hard at holding on to financial resources. They may earn a lot, but they also spend a lot. They enjoy pleasures, but they also find it important to give others a good time. Thus they can be generous to a fault. Because of this, placing them in a financial role or in a personnel position that requires strict adherence to prescribed policies would create untold stress in their lives.

Spiritual Matters

The main issues in the spiritual life of a three-tree are maturation and grounding. They have a naturally spacious quality to their being, along with an intensity which can at times manifest as chaos.

As their power of seeing is so vivid, any spiritual practices that involve visualization are excellent as a way of providing them with a focus and grounding. At the same time, because of their spacious quality, they can relate to meditations like those of Zen, that emphasize the insubstantial nature of phenomena. The use of sacred sound or mantra is beneficial for them and others as it can channel the tremendous energy they carry in their vocal system. Meditative practices and disciplines that have as their focus purification will also help the three-tree to ground and clarify their actions, speech and mental patterns.

What a three-tree must guard against in considering these practices is to be constantly chopping, changing and mixing them up. The three's interest is so wide that rather than going deep and experience fruition, they may spread themselves too thinly to accomplish much in any particular direction. If they allow themselves to go deeper, threes will be able to develop their mystical nature, the primary strength in their spiritual life.

General Health Recommendations

Three-tree people are perhaps the most agile of all the nine numbers. There is a fine relationship between their musculature and their nervous system which allows for precision, speed and grace. Thus it is that these people need to maintain a healthy level of exercise, but also need to balance this with processes of deep relaxation. Over-exertion and under-exertion can have a notable negative effect on their musculature and nervous system. There is a tendency towards sprains, muscular and connective tissue strain and damage, joint difficulties and (more nerve-related) paralysis.

The organs of the body associated with the tree/space transformation are the liver and the gall bladder. Care should be taken not to burden these organs with excess food in general and, more particularly, with foods high in oils, fats or flour products, dairy produce, alcohol, and psychoactive drugs, prescription or otherwise. Smoking cigarettes and marijuana smoking would be especially ill-advised.

Like the muscles and other organs of the body, the liver needs to be stimulated *and* allowed to rest. Three-tree people must therefore be conscious of the need for adequate rest to allow their livers to regenerate and build quality blood for the body. Late night or a nocturnal occupation is not recommended for such people. Other tree-related imbalances are listed in the profile. Of special note is the fact that as three-trees are generally over-active mentally, there is a tendency towards mental tension when under stress which can lead to various emotional and mental problems. More than likely, this will express itself in overt or repressed frustration and anger. Thus self-reflective meditation and relaxation techniques will not only help the three-tree's physical well-being, but also their mental and emotional state.

Like the four-tree person, a three-tree benefits from isometric and stretching forms of exercise. Yoga and other techniques that emphasize balances are also helpful. Progressive relaxation, autogenic training and self-hypnosis are just some of the relaxation techniques that benefit the three-tree. A diet light in animal foods and rich in complex carbohydrates, fruits and vegetables (especially greens) is recommended. Like the four-tree, a three should keep covered on windy days, especially when the wind blows from the east.

Two

◆ Profile

Number: 2

Trigram: ☷ K'un (Earth, the Receptive)

Colour: Black

Element: Earth

Internal representation: Stomach, spleen, lower half of body, flesh

Physiognomy: Abdomen

Symbolized by: Cow, mare, ant

Primary attribute: Receptive

Family member type: Mother

Management skills: Manager, Supporter – sustaining, supporting, stabilizing, holding, retaining, assimilating, anchoring, centring

Occupations: Wise woman, Shamaness, matriarch, union member, mother, obstetrician, doctor, antique and curio dealer, nurse, gardener, grocer, supermarket and bakery help, civil engineer, farmer

Illnesses: Skin disorders, blood disorders, goitre, tongue and throat symptoms, digestive tract ailments, congestion, blood sugar imbalances, depression, sense of being overwhelmed

Development enhanced by: Philanthropy, receptiveness, altruistic offering of service

Tincture: Dandelion

Best suited with: 9,6,7

Directions to travel: 6,7,9,8

Cautiousness in travelling: 1,2,3,4

◆ Narrative

In Appendix 2, I explain how each number in succession, from greatest to smallest, represents an increasingly contracting (yang) force in the space-time continuum. Thus, as the cycle of years moves from nine to one (see Figure 26, page 167), people experience an increased sense of speed and intensity in their lives. (It is also true that as the number nine year comes round again, people will, in general, experience more ease.) Interestingly enough, as if to counter-balance this effect, one of the primary characteristics of two-earth is that it is the most receptive (yin) of all the nine numbers.

To clarify this seeming paradox in terms of the maturation process of which it is part in the Five Transformation Theory, it is almost as if whatever has budded (tree transformation) and blossomed (fire transformation) begins to take on its first appearance as a mature entity. This is a bold step in the cycle from creation to dissolution. It is no surprise therefore that two-earth people exhibit the qualities of tenaciousness and strong will (even stubbornness), yet also mildness, kindness and gentleness. They manifest both the yang intensity and the yin receptivity of the time.

Two-earth is considered the primal mother number (as six-metal is the primal father number). As such, whether male or female, there is a distinctly feminine quality to this person's way of being. They feel an intimate connection with their environment and strive to maintain order in whatever they are involved in. They can be somewhat old fashioned and conservative in their endeavours and are workers rather than innovators.

Being caring and hard-working, if a two-earth throws a party, they are very concerned about how things look and feel for others. They will try to maintain the right atmosphere for their guests, and will busily flit around making sure that their guests are having a good time and have enough to eat and drink. In such circumstances (and also more generally) they may appear as social butterflies, somewhat superficial in their brief encounters with those they feel they are attending to. However, ask a two-earth how such a party or event went and they will be able to tell you what was going on with each and every person with whom they had contact. Their powers of observation can be exceedingly keen. Unlike the caring quality inherent in the other earth numbers, five and eight, the two-earth's care focuses on a general sense of well-being rather than the specific issues and problems in other people's lives. Thus their attention and caring tends to be more unconditional and constant.

Although one could call a two-earth person more of a generalist as regards their observation and learning, they do like to take note of the details. They can be as interested in the operations of a machine as they are in the dynamics of a relationship. At the same time, the details don't actually matter to them very much, even though they may exhibit an obsessive interest in them. It's as though they are hungry for as much as they can know of what is happening, but really only want to get the general drift of things. Others may consider this to be superficial. Twos learn quickly and forget quickly, but ever so much want to be helpful and a part of whatever is going on. For a two-earth anything worth doing is worth doing *now*.

A two-earth's energies are best focused when they are part of some larger plan or part of a group. They are not leaders but joiners, and they remain faithful to any group they join. They are not initiators or self-starters, but given a task, they will go at it with a tenacity not seen in the other numbers. Like a good mother, they will care for and look after the tasks and needs of the group, even in the face of great difficulties. If left to their own devices, they get bored and are somewhat at a loss for a sense of purpose.

Although best within a group, two-earths need overt acknowledgement of their achievements. Whatever they are doing, they want to let others know how it is going. If some level of acknowledgement is not forthcoming, they are thrown back upon themselves and become self-doubting. They may be envious of the attention others receive and, as a result, may be quite callous, if not vicious, towards such people. Two-earths usually make it harder on themselves in this respect in that they like to associate either with people older than themselves or with people that they rate as 'somebody'. Thus they may also exhibit a tendency to try to fit in by putting on airs. In the long run, such behaviour has an undermining effect on them, making them retreat to safer, more secure ground. Thus, in times of personal stress, a two-earth may prefer to stick to what they know rather than venture out and risk failure. Such periods are short-lived, however, they can easily let go of their envy, pull themselves up and go in search of another task or group into which they can pour their energy.

Love Relationships

The primary emphasis in a love relationship for a two-earth person is to be able to lavish their care and love on others. Such an attitude naturally attracts people to them. However, their willingness to display such care and affection may at times be interpreted as a sexual invitation, especially if the two-earth is female. This is not necessarily the case. Two-earths do enjoy sexual involvement, but it is just one of the many ways they employ to demonstrate their care for their partners. The men of this number are generally liked by women because of their care and consideration. The women of this number will usually be drawn to men who are strong, athletic and in some way powerful. When she finds the man of her liking, a two-earth woman will be fairly direct in letting him know. If a man in whom she has no interest approaches her, she will set him straight in an instant.

Two-earths get into trouble in relationships when they display their tendency to be obsessive over the details of their partner's life. They may also try to be everyone and everything for their partner. In such a case, sex may become a dutiful act, performed to please. Thus a two-earth needs to be able to distinguish between devotion and co-dependence. If they do not assess this periodically, they run the risk of their partner feeling suffocated by their affections and attentions.

In general, this is a person who will be a devoted and faithful partner, whose unconditional love and caring can be both moving and inspiring both to their partner and to others around them. Still, they are well-advised to watch their obsessive tendencies, as well as over-reliance on their partner. Both of those tendencies may lead to unexpected separation.

Business Relationships

This is a person who cares. As part of a group or organization two-earths will immerse themselves in the tasks, functions and relationships. They like to be a part of the team. Organizations in which they work best are public or service-oriented. They may also be found in volunteer positions. Fields of work and positions that will create stress for them are those that are scientific or technical in nature, as the precision that is demanded can be mentally and physically taxing on the two-earth.

As part of a team, in the role of a supporter rather than a director, the two-earth person will avidly dive into tasks and will work consistently until they are completed. They have a sense of how systems work and can develop routines to keep things moving along. But they will need direction. Don't assume that when they say they understand they really do. A well laid-out plan is useful for the two-earth to have in front of them. With good supervision and support from fellow workers, the two-earth will create products of superior quality.

On a personal level, a happy, purposeful two-earth person creates bonds and a sense of caring. Their team spirit can be contagious and they are skilled at teaching others what needs to be done. Problems arise when, out of a sense of insecurity or jealousy, they create rivalries. When balanced, however, the two-earth wants to be involved with the team and with fellow workers. They will probably find themselves listening to co-workers' problems and concerns. They therefore do not do well in a supervisory capacity. The idea of having to hire, fire, or judge others is contrary to their unconditional caring nature. Put a two-earth person in such a position and you will have a person that may appear to be doing the task at hand, as they do want to please those in authority. But in doing so, they may be experiencing endless worry, sleepless nights and self-doubt.

As regards finances, two-earths are frugal and tend to accumulate steadily. They do not speculate. Thus they can be good at watching and balancing the books. On a personal level, however, they may find that when touched by someone else's need they are over-generous and thus place themselves in financial difficulties. Still, little harm comes from such generosity. Money may come to them in unexpected ways. A two-earth's financial practices may be less extreme than the five-earth's – more modestly fortunate or unfortunate.

Spiritual Matters

Service to others is the trademark of two-earth people. And to clarify this virtue so that it arises more out of altruism, the two-earth needs to address any self-doubt or sense of deep sadness that they may be harbouring. These two factors, if allowed to cloud the two-earth's world view, may create cynicism, jealousy or even contempt of others. Thus they need to work on cultivating greater confidence in themselves.

To do this, a two-earth should find others who have committed themselves to the spiritual values and path they wish to tread. Because of their devotional nature and team mentality, they can be examples of spiritual or religious discipline, but they need to know the difference between faith and blind adherence.

Compassion is strong with such people, yet they need to be able to distinguish between true compassion and 'idiot compassion' or co-dependence. Rather than just giving because they want to or think they should, a two-earth must pay more attention to the real needs of others so that they can truly benefit the people they are serving. If they do not give this more thought, they may find that they are rebuffed more than appreciated for what they do.

Self-empowerment practices and meditations are advised. The use of music and chanting would be useful. If they can overcome doubt and become confident in their service and compassion, the unconditional nature of the two-earth can be a powerful force in clearing away obstacles in life for themselves and the people around them.

General Health Recommendations

Two-earth people have a difficult time accepting that they need to be pro-active in their health. With so many others in need they may feel that they have no time to pay attention to themselves, and may feel they do not deserve other people's interest in their health. They may even go so far as to refuse help. But two-earth people must come to realize (usually with help from kind yet persistent friends), that they can best serve noble causes if they take care of themselves. Usually a two-earth will reluctantly give in to such logic, but once they have given in, they are quick to feel the benefits of a pro-active health programme.

Most two-earth people will tend to be plump rather than slender. Food and earthy sustenance may be of either constant or little interest to such folk. Thus they may be gourmands and eat excessively, or they may eat very little, but make poor choices in what they eat. Of the foods they are attracted to when out of balance energetically, it is such things as sugars and other refined foods, alcohol and stimulants such as caffeine that they will indulge in excessively. Such foods are difficult for them to metabolize. Hypoglycaemia, blood sugar imbalances and problems related to bad dietary habits can lead to blood and lymph disorders. If the two-earth is over-extended emotionally by becoming over-involved in other people's problems, self-doubt, deep sadness and possible depression will ensue. Add to this a diet that is stressful and the two-earth can suffer even more depression, fatigue and immune-related diseases.

Two-earth people need to eat sensibly, particularly avoiding refined carbohydrate, alcoholic beverages, caffeinated drinks and 'junk food'. They need to exercise and stay active. Exercise processes that particularly facilitate blood and lymphatic cleansing are recommended. Mini-trampolines and inversion machines are useful devices for the two-earth. They would also benefit from the occasional Swedish or lymphatic style of massage. If they are to get involved in processes of relaxation or meditation, it is best that they incorporate meaningful thoughts and prayers that allow them to feel that the quiet moments they take to recharge themselves also benefit others.

One

◆ Profile

Number: 1

Trigram: ☵ K'an (Water, the Abysmal)

Colour: White

Element: Water

Internal representation: Kidneys, bladder, sex organs, bones, nervous system

Physiognomy: Ear

Symbolized by: Pig, rat, fox, bat

Primary attribute: Hardship, danger

Family member type: Middle Son

Management skills: Yin: The Allocator – containing, setting limits, storing, allocating resources, delineating boundaries, managing resources

Yang: The Motivator – generating, regulating, motivating, energizing, providing direction, reflecting, risk-analysis

Occupations: Social worker, printing and dyeing, fishing industry, chemist, massage therapist, philosopher, writer, dairy worker, oilman, restaurant owner, waiter, bartender, lawyer, maintenance person

Illnesses: Kidney ailments, earache, venereal disease, melancholia, abnormal menses, haemorrhoids, neurasthenia, paranoia

Development enhanced by: Baptism, purification practices

Tincture: Skullcap

Best suited with: 6,7,3,4

Directions to travel: 6,7,3,4

Cautiousness in travelling: 1,2,8,9

◆ Narrative

One-water represents the end of the nine-year descending spiral through time. The word 'spiral' is used here rather than 'cycle' because it points to the fact that while the energetics of what comes around through time bear similar characteristics and appear the same, history does *not* in fact repeat itself. Something new is always added, albeit in keeping with the dynamics of the transformations present. A cycle is a closed circuit. A spiral is open-ended, but moves in a cycle-like path.

The water transformation phase is associated with winter. What has been created, developed and matured now experiences its own dissolution. Winter is a time of year when life recedes deep into the ground, and movement is subtle, if present at all, while the thaw of spring is awaited.

Thus the one-water is a deep-thinking person who is rather enigmatic. There is a quality of solitude that pervades their being. In social situations, usually to ease those around them, they may appear chatty and superficial. They will generally not say what is on their minds as their natural brilliance takes them to deeper and more subtle levels than they expect others to be able to understand. Although generally correct in this assumption, it nevertheless needs close scrutiny, as this attitude can lead them to be opinionated and contemptuous of others. The enigmatic aura that they project even while in conversation can make others feel a bit uncertain as to what the one-water is really about. People may try to be liked by one-waters for fear of becoming the subject of their disdain. Thus, one-water people need to be more skilful with, and develop more equanimity about, their opinions, lest they be viewed as bigots.

Because they keep their deepest thoughts and plans to themselves, one-water people's actions will often seem abrupt and
sudden, even though they have been planning things for some
time. Ask a one-water person a question that involves consideration and you may have to wait some time before the answer bobs
to the surface. Ironically, although deep-thinking, if they are put
into a position where what is going on is not known or familiar to
them and they have not been able to formulate their opinions
clearly, one-water people may find themselves swept along by the
momentum of the situation. Thus, they can fall prey to a herd or
mob mentality, something they will tend to regret deeply once
they have a chance to settle down and be more reflective. Their
natural wilfulness is so intense that in such circumstances, having
made a sudden change of direction, the one-water finds it difficult
to maintain equilibrium.

Although water has its own inherent properties, its location,
force and movement is dependent upon the circumstances
around it. Thus a one-water displays a fluid adaptability. Regardless of the circumstances, a one-water can fit in and play the part,
and will usually do so whether they like it or not. When their
attention and personal involvement is demanded in situations not
to their liking, they will reluctantly perform as required, lying and
flattering if necessary just to keep things superficially satisfactory.

Because they are sensitive to the effects of their environment
and circumstances, and because of their natural fluidity, one-
waters usually experience life as somewhat constrained but always
changing. They need to strive hard to know themselves because
their life experience is constantly shifting. Their superficial ways
conceal a deeper desire to come to terms with the significance of
all the happenings in their life. They need to develop and maintain
a well-defined detachment to accomplish this. Their insights can
be furthered by paying more attention to what others have to say,
something which does not come easily to them. If they cannot
come around to a more detached view of life, they will constantly
experience upset and every change will be viewed as one more
hardship to endure.

The one-water person may appear as sad or meekly reserved.
Yet they have a thirst for life and living. They appear drab or
rather colourless, particularly in their dress but they actually
enjoy being colourful and can bring up from their depths a

vivaciousness which is absolutely magnetizing. Although they can be disdainful of others and appear judgemental or withdrawn on social occasions, still the experience of being at such a gathering means a lot to them at a deeper level. For, although one-waters like solitude, they do not like to be excluded or isolated. If a one-water can draw up and project even a glimpse of joy in a situation, not only will this bring delight to others, but as it is reflected back to them, it will begin to permeate more of their experiences.

The fluidity of a one-water will create a life that is varied and challenging. These people will usually find that their circumstances change a lot. Family, finances and overall security continually change for them and if they resist or deny such change, freezing up rather than 'going with the flow', they risk creating unnecessary stress for themselves. One-waters may also find themselves moving or travelling frequently in their lifetime. It is only natural for such people to be cautious in their undertakings, in a sense trying to stem the tide of the ebb and flow in their life. To resist or deny such change and movement, however, will create in them a fear of life that can be paralysing and cause stress and dis-ease.

Love Relationships

Although one-water people enjoy solitude, they want to feel free to *choose* to be alone. Thus there is no contradiction in the fact that they may like companionship. However, companionship to them is not necessarily defined as doing something with their partner. The companion to a one-water needs to be like a vessel or a cup. The cup contains, but is not a part of, the water. Thus, the one-water's partner must get used to the idea that they are with but not necessarily a part of the one-water's life.

This does not mean that such a person should feel discounted or any less significant in the one-water person's life. One-waters are not people to choose partners lightly. They ask questions, check attributes, reflect deeply about the person they are considering as a partner. Once committed, they settle in and hold on. They may, on the surface, act unperturbed or nonchalant, but underneath they possess a love which runs deep.

If the involvement is sexual, the bond between one-waters and their partners is even more powerful as the exchange of sexual energy is one of the primary ways in which one-waters learn more about themselves and deepen their spirituality. Because of this, there may be a tendency to over-emphasize sex in their lives, either by minimizing or exaggerating its importance. If they are sexually rebuffed or disappointed, one-waters may rigidly abstain from sexual involvement. On the other hand, they may have such a strong sex drive that their passions are animalistic. The men of this number may act like gigolos, while the women maintain an entourage of several lovers or conjure ways of experiencing sexual pleasure. Because a one-water's experience of sexuality runs so deep, and as sexual identity and security are often major issues in the lives of other people, a one-water's personal knowledge and expertise in this area of life makes them good as counsellors for both men and women.

A lesson one-waters should learn in their love relationships is detachment. Once involved, especially sexually, one-water people can be extremely possessive. As a result, they may not only lose their own sense of self-identity, but also sacrifice or neglect other important relationships in their lives. They also have a tendency to be excessively lavish with money and gifts and thus can heedlessly squander whatever savings they have accumulated. Such behaviour often comes about when the one-water fears being abandoned.

One-waters must come to terms with the fact that their need for solitude is best satisfied when they recognize how companionship can create the support necessary for that need to be met. Being more verbal in communicating their appreciation and love for their partner will not only create a greater sense of closeness, but will also possibly alleviate their tendency to cling. If such issues are not addressed, one-waters and their partners may be locked in a relationship for years; the one-waters feeling isolated and misunderstood, their partners feeling trapped.

Business Relationships

Because they are cautious and thoughtful about matters that are important to them, one-water people are excellent in roles that require clear, succinct communication within an organization. They can often paraphrase a vast array of verbiage into a form that just makes the point. However, they can go too far in this respect, cutting back excessively and then expecting people to understand complex concepts with just a few words. In such instances, the enigmatic or cryptic response the one-water person gives may seem very powerful, but what exactly is meant is not clear to anyone but themselves. It is therefore important for them to be receptive enough to be able to elaborate when necessary, and to do so in a way which does not convey disdain.

The one-water person is not a team player in the sense that a two-earth is. They are loners, but generally rely on having some context in which they can operate independently. Consequently, they are excellent at setting limits and establishing boundaries within an organizational structure.

As water nourishes most of what exists on this planet, so it is that one-water people nourish the organizations of which they are part. They energize situations and help keep staff moving. Thus they may be useful in management positions or in some capacity that involves establishing the direction of a plan. They are excellent in developing mission statements and mapping out the interconnections of all the various sub-components of a situation. This does not mean, however, that the one-water person should be viewed as an administrator, for detail can be quite tedious for such people. They are not good at looking for new ideas, but rather for new connections in what is already in place.

Nor are one-waters suited to positions where they are actively involved in the completion of tasks as a primary responsibility. Their forte is reflecting upon what has gone before and bringing their deep insights to bear on the present so that plans for the future may be steered in more meaningful directions. It must be borne in mind, however, that for them meaningfulness will not be determined by other people or by an organization, but by their own experiences. If one-waters find what they are involved with meaningless, they are likely to drop their involvement or just leave. What a one-water needs to guard against is over-reacting in these situations. There are times when they worry too much about things and take tasks or situations to unnecessary depths.

One-water people also do not handle positions which involve heavy physical labour very well, either because they are too frail or sensitive, or because they find such work unacceptable. Of course they will do the work if necessary, but they will somehow convey to those around them that it is not to their liking.

Financially, a one-water has neither excessively good nor excessively bad fortune. They don't amass much wealth personally, but they get by. In a business context, especially, where risks are involved and the competition is slick, it is best not to have a one-water involved in transactions as they can easily be swindled. They have a tendency to be impressed by big displays of power and money. This is especially true if the person they are negotiating with is of the opposite sex. At the same time, where resources other than money are involved, their cautiousness allows them to apportion those resources so as to sustain them in the long term. They are generally conscious of their own limitations.

Spiritual Matters

Because of their deep-thinking nature, it is *meaning* that plays a central role in the one-water's spiritual life. Life's events come fast and furious to them and it is a challenge in their life to learn *and* let go, almost simultaneously.

To be present and relax into the moment as it is, a one-water needs to go through a baptism or purification process – to clean things up and not hold on. Humour is an attribute to cultivate as it is too easy for one-waters to find themselves being too serious about the significance of things and holding on to matters and issues in their life unnecessarily. As they let go more and 'go with the flow', their insights become easier to communicate.

One-water people, because of their depth and sensitivity, have an innate sense of the human condition. Although they can appear condescending to others, much of this behaviour comes from almost caring too much for people. With more detachment, this way of being can be transformed into an active compassion, and will be like soothing waters for those to whom they turn their attention.

Relaxation and silent meditation are helpful. Having bowls of water on a shrine or altar is grounding, also the use of sound, especially crystal bowls or chimes. Meditation on compassion should be emphasized. As sexuality can be an important factor in spiritual development, one-waters who have practised various purifications and spiritual disciplines may wish to investigate the Tao of Love or consult an authentic master regarding tantric sexual practice.

General Health Recommendations

One-water people must learn to take care of their bladder-kidney energy, along with associated tissues, structures and functions, like the skeletal structure and the reproductive system (see profile). Such people are more prone to problems with sexual organs. Women may have gynaecological difficulties, irregular menses, etc., while men may have prostate problems, and possibly impotence at times.

These are people who need to take care not to get too cold. Adequate warmth around the stomach, middle and lower back and ears is recommended. Such people need to keep good-quality water and salt as basics in their food preparation. Salt-covered snacks and the salting of foods at the table are not recommended. Nor should food be too hot or too cold. Macrobiotic food preparation and observances should be investigated.

Because of their sensitivity, one-water people are prone to nervous irritation, which usually expresses itself as fear, even paranoia when under extreme duress. A stressed one-water may express a timidity that makes them immobile or rigid, like ice. This can, in turn, have negative effects on all the physiological aspects mentioned earlier. Progressive relaxation can be useful to this person, as is soothing asynchronous music which allows the mind to settle. A one-water would also benefit from right and left brain exercises. Such practices and observances are useful to the one-water over their lifetime as unbridled tension and stress may lead them to become senile in later years.

Exercise should be aimed at keeping the skeletal system flexible, especially the spine. Yoga would be an excellent choice as would swimming, preferably in salt water or pools that use ozone or oyster shell for purification rather than chlorine.

Part III

◆

EVALUATING NUMBER COMBINATIONS

◆

The Houses

As I said in Part 1, both the natal month and the natal year numbers will migrate to different houses in the Magic Square over time. Since each number represents a particular transformation phase, as does each house, there is a mix of qualities which can be complementary, supportive, confrontative or conflicting in nature. Thus we go through our lives learning to adjust to ever-changing circumstances which have, at the same time, a certain level of regularity or order. As we become familiar with our experiences in each one of the houses and begin to pay more attention to where our natal numbers are in time, we have the advantage of knowing to some extent what to expect, and can modify our behaviour and interactions accordingly.

Besides the knowledge we gain from understanding transformation and elemental mixes, the houses are also used for directiono-

Figure 11. The Magic Square showing the houses and their transformation phases

	SE	S	SW
	House of **4** TREE	House of **9** FIRE	House of **2** EARTH
E	House of **3** TREE	House of **5** FIRE	House of **7** EARTH	W
	House of **8** TREE	House of **1** FIRE	House of **6** EARTH
	NE	N	NW

logy. For although our natal numbers migrate, the houses remain stationary, as do the compass directions they represent. As this volume is not about directionology or systems of geomancy, only general recommendations as to adverse and positive directions for travel are listed in the profile. Briefly, if a number is positive for a person, wherever that number is on the Magic Square will be a positive direction for that person to travel at that time. The exception to this is when either the natal month or the natal year number is in the House of Five. At such times, travelling is generally not recommended.

A person studying Nine Star Ki should try to familiarize themselves with the impact the houses have on their natal month and year numbers. *In particular, one should pay attention to the house that the child number was in at the time of birth and the House of Five, which is where the adult number always resides at the time of birth.*

Thus it is important for everyone to understand the House of Five, as it impacts on all adult natal number potentials. It will, therefore, be discussed first. All other house numbers will then be discussed briefly, including a general way of viewing the transformation mixes that occur as the child numbers occupy a given house at birth. House descriptions are dynamic, describing what one may experience as one's numbers pass through them. As regards one's natal month number, the impact of the given house it resided in at the time of birth will be more of a constant or pervasive factor in one's life, during childhood and especially when under stress. Descriptions will be metaphoric in the sense that they will use the Five Transformations concepts of mother –son, the cycle of regeneration and the ko or cycle of control, and present them in a psychological format. Such patterns and mixes are subtle, yet significant in our relationships in the world, so I would recommend you to delve deeper into Five Transformations theory for greater understanding and appreciation.

◆ The House of Five

The House of Five is depicted as a house of danger, of alluring powers and upheavals. It is also considered a house in which either very fortunate or very unfortunate circumstances can arise. Looked at with a greater introspection, the energetics that we are presented with when our natal numbers occupy the House of Five are more appropriately viewed as karmic reckoning: what has been sown over time is reaped now. This can be positive or negative, but is usually a very accurate fruition of what has gone before, particularly over the previous eight years.

At the time of our birth, the number of the year (and month, if our natal month number is the same as our natal year number) in which we were born resides in the House of Five. On a basic energetic level, this will mean that we must understand what the mix is between the transformation phase of our natal year (or month) and the earth quality of the House of Five. The House of Five in itself, however, is representative of a precarious balance between expanding and contracting forces. On a personal level, this means that the characteristics of the number residing in the House of Five will present themselves in the broadest possible way, even to extremes – from the most altruistic behaviour to the most egocentric. From a more balanced perspective, what is being addressed here is how one learns to be out in the world and, at the same time, take care of oneself.

We need to balance self-nurturing with service to others and the world around us in order to develop our adult natal potentials fully. The service we render to others depends on the varying characteristics of the natal numbers. Nurturing has to do with recognizing what it is that we need to take care of ourselves so that our service to others does not become crippling. We do not need to balance service and nurturing evenly. It is more a question of being mature and sensitive enough to know what our potentials are and how to maximize them. An ability to be introspective is necessary if self-nurturing is not to become self-indulgence and service is not to become martyrdom. When a person knows what balance is right for them, they are self-actualizing. As they self-actualize, a true altruism naturally emerges that is enlivening for all concerned.

When a person is actualizing their adult natal number potentials in their life, they may tend to express some of the characteristics of the House of Five. Thus the manner in which a person acts may be misconstrued as arrogant and self-centred or timid and self-effacing. Such an erroneous view has something to do with projection; their success reflects back to others the struggle they themselves experience.

Every nine years, when the current year puts all numbers back into the configuration they were in at our birth, we come face to face with what our potentials are and the developments of the previous eight years as measured against them. We can see how we have done and how we are doing. Are we taking care of our needs? Do we feel empowered in our interactions in the world? If we have been careless in our relationships and interactions, there is a strong likelihood that we will have to face that fact at this time. If we have been working towards a greater integration of our needs and potentials, our work will come to fruition at this time.

In either case, during the time when our natal year comes back into the House of Five, it is best to reflect, assess, accept and plan for the future based on what we have gleaned from our experiences and where we now want to go in our lives. This is not a year for action, however, and travelling or making any radical shifts in what we are doing is ill-advised. However, because it is such a challenging time, it can be quite difficult to face oneself truthfully. There may even be a tendency to become frenetically busy, as if wriggling in the energetics of the time. Nevertheless, the best thing one can do is to be mindful and allow oneself to relax into the experience of being with oneself. In quietness and reflection, one can then lay plans or try to project where one wants to be in the next nine years and what one needs to reach those goals. Such plans will then be activated in the following year. To attempt to initiate new projects or ideas at this time is ill-advised.

It must be remembered that while we have a dominant natal month and year number, we possess within our make-up aspects of all nine numbers in varying degrees. As all numbers migrate over time and must thus pass through the House of Five, there will be times when the different aspects of our being need to be more carefully scrutinized. Next to our natal year, our natal month number will be the most significant in the House of Five. During those times we may find that childhood issues are confronted, as well as how well we have overcome various levels of co-dependence on the world. As with the natal year, it is wise to take some time to reflect quietly on those aspects of our lives. Like the natal year number, when the natal month number resides in the House of Five, one should plan but not initiate changes. Also, travelling may cause stress and imbalances that take a long time to overcome.

Apart from the migration of numbers into the House of Five on a yearly basis, they also migrate monthly. Within each year, therefore, our natal month and year numbers will also enter the House of Five, and at these times it is best to stay put and reflect upon the issues that our numbers bring up for us.

During the times when our natal year or month enter the House of Five, especially in the cycle of nine years, our health is more greatly challenged. *The Anthology of I Ching* suggests that it is a time when we should be alert to digestive difficulties, heart complaints, immune-related diseases, even cerebral hemorrhages.[5] One possible explanation for this is that during such times we may become destabilized as we are asked to come to grips with ourselves emotionally.

The Five Year in the House of Five:

Every nine years the five year enters its own house. Historically, such years are challenging times. The years 1914 and 1941 saw the world massively preoccupied with war. In the recent history of the United States, the Korean War was in 1950 and the Tet Offensive in Vietnam was in 1968. The beginning of 1986 was heralded by the explosion of the space shuttle Challenger. Others may wish to investigate the history of other countries to see whether the five year has produced major events that shaped or were an expression of the times.

What is significant on a personal level is that all numbers reside in their own houses, that is three sits in the House of Three, six in the House of Six, and so on. Consequently, what each of us experience is our own primal forces in their most dynamic or raw state. In particular, both our adult and our child natal number qualities become accentuated. Thus it is made painfully clear how we are handling these aspects of our lives, as well as all the qualities that make up our character from the other numbers. It is a time when we can feel rather alone. Therefore a sense of separation between individuals, cultures, societies and nations can become exaggerated. A five month can create a similar effect, but not as dramatically or with as much force as the five year. Such a year can be as potent, as regards self-examination and transformation, as when our own natal year or month is in the House of Five, if not more so.

Such times demand stillness and reflection if we are to work with them successfully. Unfortunately the rawness of the times may invoke tendencies to project and needlessly initiate turmoil and conflict. Perhaps if the energetics of these times are understood more clearly, individuals and nations will be able to examine things more closely, review actions and plan ways of overcoming rather than creating division. It is a potent time to come up with new strategies and solutions to old problems as well as focusing on aspirations for the future.

◆ The Other Houses: Some General Guidelines

Before looking more specifically at the other houses and their energetics, there are some general guidelines that are useful for further interpretations. These guidelines are based on principles from the Law of Five Transformations; the mother–son relationships, and the cycle of ko or energetic controls. Naboru Muramoto's *Healing Ourselves* is, once again, an excellent source for studying these concepts further.

The mother–son relationship has to do with how one transformation or element feeds and nurtures another. Each transformation will be the child of one transformation and the mother of another. Thus:

tree/space (3,4) is the child of water (1) and
tree/space (3,4) is the mother of fire (9);
fire (9) is the child of tree/space (3,4) and
fire (9) is the mother of earth (2,5,8);
earth (2,5,8) is the child of fire (9) and
earth (2,5,8) is the mother of metal/air (6,7);
metal/air (6,7) is the child of earth (2,5,8) and
metal/air (6,7) is the mother of water (1);
water (1) is the child of metal/air (6,7) and
water (1) is the mother of tree/space (3,4).

The cycle of ko is also the cycle of death. As things in nature move towards death, their path of deterioration is in a certain progression through the Five Transformations. This cycle is also called a cycle of control, for when any particular transformation is radically excessive or deficient in the balance of healthy life

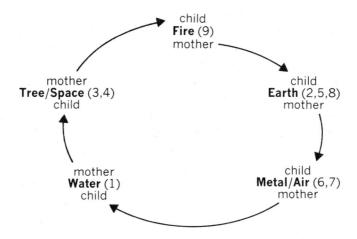

Figure 12. The cycle of regeneration

forms, that excess or deficiency has a direct effect on another transformation. The relationship between transformations and the transformations they control are as follows:

tree/space (3,4)	controls	earth (2,5,8)
earth (2,5,8)	,,	water (1)
water (1)	,,	fire (9)
fire (9)	,,	metal/air (6,7)
metal/air	,,	tree/space (3,4)

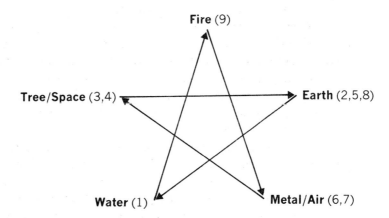

Figure 13. The ko or control cycle

Unless the child or natal month number is the same as the adult natal year number, it will reside in one of the other eight houses in the Magic Square. To find the house that the child number resides in refer to the Universal Chart that has the adult natal year number that you are looking at in the centre (House of Five). Depending on the relationship of the natal month transformation and the transformation of the house that it resides in at the time of birth, a person will experience their childhood, periods of dependency, and stress in particular ways that have to do with the mix of these two transformations. There are two aspects of this mix. On a basic level, there are the factors of the mother–son and ko cycle in the Law of Five Transformations that will be the source of *general attitudes*. On a subtler level, there will be the actual qualities of the transformations/elements involved that create the *character* or the way in which these general attitudes are projected from a personality. As regards the actual transformations/elements involved, what one will also observe is that before the stress and imbalance patterns of the natal month transformation emerge, the physiological and psychological characteristics inherent in the particular house that it resides in will be activated.

For example, let us assume that a 4 adult, 9 child is experiencing stress. As the 9 child resides in the House of One-Water, such a person will probably experience the fear and cautiousness of the water transformation and possibly even manifest such stress symptoms as low back pain, prostate or genital/urinary tract problems before experiencing the anxiety characteristic of a nine-fire.

Thus experiencing the characteristics or symptoms of the house that the child natal number resides in can be a useful way of recognizing that one is entering into a stress mode, or that childhood or dependency patterns have been activated. Therefore, when examining the characteristics of the child natal month transformation, you need to consider the house that the child natal month number resides in.

This of course requires some degree of finesse in understanding Five Transformation theory. However, when it comes to the more basic attitudes the person will be experiencing, there are some useful metaphors regarding houses, mother–son relationship and control cycle patterns that can be used as rules of thumb before deeper investigation.

Apart from the impact that the House of Five has on our adult natal number at the time of birth, there are basically six ways, described further on in this chapter, in which the mother–son relationship and the ko cycle reveal themselves in the relationship between the child month natal number and the house that it resides in at the time of birth.

There are two ways in which you can find out which house the child natal number resides in at the time of birth. First, use the calculation methods recommended in Part 1. Find the Universal Chart that has the required natal year number in the centre (the House of Five). On that chart, look for the natal month number. It will be in a particular house, the number of which you can identify by referring to the Magic Square at the beginning of this chapter (Figure 11). Figure 9 and the accompanying example on page 20 will give you an idea of how to do it.

The second method involves calculating the natal year and month numbers and then finding that combination on the Easy Reference Table (Figure 10, page 25). This table will also show you in which of the six ways the natal month numbers and the houses relate to each other, so making it easier for you to go directly to the most relevant relationship on the pages that follow. Of course, you could also go through the six descriptions and locate the particular month and house configurations you are looking for by scanning the combination listings provided.

In the headings that follow, the numbers in parentheses are the child natal month numbers and the numbers spelled out are the houses.

When the child natal number is the mother to the transformation of the house that it resides in: (3) nine, (4) nine, (9) two, (9) five, (9) eight, (2) six, (2) seven, (5) six, (5) seven, (8) six, (8) seven, (6) one, (7) one, (1) three, (1) four

When the mother comes to visit the son, she usually has opinions about how he is living. When a person has a child natal number that is the mother to the transformation of the house that the child number resides in, they will usually be over-vigilant, preoccupied with their surroundings, and more opinionated than people with other configurations. Such people need to be aware of their over-critical predisposition. Their expectations may be higher than those around them, as may be their levels of elation or disappointment.

When the child natal number is the son to the transformation of the house that it resides in: (3) one, (4) one, (9) three, (9) four, (2) nine, (5) nine, (8) nine, (6) two, (6) five, (6) eight, (7) two, (7) five, (7) eight, (1) six, (1) seven

Here is a situation where a person may have difficulty breaking from their dependency and childhood patterns. In this particular configuration, it is as if the child does not have enough inner strength to move out of the house. Thus in childhood or when under stress, such a person may feel complacent about their situation. They may complain about life's experiences, yet have little motivation to take any concrete steps towards changing things. At times others may want to shake such a person up, a desire which in many cases is appropriate, as these people have a limited view of their potential.

When the child natal number is in the house of the transformation it controls: (3) two, (3) five, (3) eight, (4) two, (4) five, (4) eight, (9) six, (9) seven, (2) one, (5) one, (8) one, (6) three, (6) four, (7) three, (7) four, (1) nine

When an element is out of balance dramatically, it has a stifling effect on the transformation that it controls. However, in this particular situation there is a more unfamiliar dynamic. Here the transformation that would normally be in control is being contained by the transformation it controls.

Metaphorically speaking, the child is living in a house where it is being constrained, almost against its will or natural tendencies. The result is a person who in childhood, or under stress when the child natal number is activated, tends to be rebellious or explosive. There is a constant urge to assert themselves in order to shed their feelings of being trapped. Thus the abruptness or emotional response this person has when confronted with unpleasant experiences has more to do with internal psychological mechanisms than a clear response to outside stimulation; hence the response can be disproportionate to what the situation actually warrants. A person who understands this aspect of themselves is less likely to blame or alienate others at such moments.

When the child natal number is in the house of the transformation by which it is controlled: (3) six, (3) seven, (4) six, (4) seven, (9) one, (2) three, (2) four, (5) three, (5) four, (8) three, (8) four, (6) nine, (7) nine, (1) two, (1) five, (1) eight

Here is a situation where the child, or person in stress feels rightly controlled. There is a tendency towards resignation, a feeling of 'This is how it is and why should it be any different?' This should not be viewed as complacency, however, as when the child natal number resides in the mother's house. Here, there can be more of a sense of resentment, as well as a strong desire to break free. Whereas the child residing in the mother's house may need some prodding, the person in this situation needs support as they strive to overcome 'impossibility' thinking.

When the child natal month number and the adult natal year number are the same: (1) one, (2) two, (3) three, (4) four, (5) five, (6) six, (7) seven, (8) eight, (9) nine

Here is a situation where, at the time of birth, the child and adult number both reside in the House of Five. Regardless of the transformation of the number, therefore, the energetics of five-earth and the House of Five must be viewed as strong factors in the person's life.

The lives of such individuals seem constant. Whereas for others, at the end of the second cycle of nine or when there is a move towards greater independence, the experience is one of making a shift from one energetic to another, there is no such transition here. Life just goes on feeling the way it always has been. Thus childhood patterns are carried over into adult life. Dealing with authority may be like dealing with one's mother and father. Because one transformation only is represented there is seemingly no contrast in experience. Thus it can be difficult for such a person to understand someone else's point of view, or to conceive of someone experiencing life in any other way than the way they themselves experience it. Thus such people can be stubborn and seemingly arrogant.

This configuration also means that their strengths are their weaknesses. Because of the strong House of Five dominance they can be uncertain about themselves and overdo things. If they remain balanced however, they will have all the positive qualities of the transformation plus the energy of the five-earth house.

On the physical level, it is more than likely that such a person will be hypoglycaemic. The dietary guidance and stress management techniques recommended for their particular transformation should be used. Psychoactive substances can be particularly injurious to such people.

When the child natal number resides in the house that is the same as its own transformation, but not the same as its adult natal number: (2) five, (2) eight, (3) four, (4) three, (5) two, (5) eight, (6) seven, (7) six, (8) two, (8) five

Because the energetic of the house is a more yin or yang aspect of the same transformation as the child natal month number, a person might experience a sense of wholeness from this combination. Such a person may have a generally relaxed demeanour – they may even appear to be masterful when handling stress. Rather than trying to change situations if they are not in keeping with what they want, such people may be more willing to work with things as they are. Thus they may be very compliant in most circumstances.

It is only because we are focusing on the relationship between the child natal number and the houses that the more challenging aspects of these relationships are being looked at. Such challenges should not be viewed as either good or bad. Rather, when in childhood, or later when stress re-evokes childhood patterns, the struggle from dependence and co-dependency towards independence must take into account the house and the house/natal number factor. This is also true for the natal year number, but in the case of the child natal month number, there is more of a sense of history to work through.

Looked at more objectively each house has the potential to support growth and maturation. As a number migrates into a particular house it becomes a matter of seizing the moment, taking from the situation what it offers. From the child natal month perspective, such a situation offers us the opportunity to loosen our fixation on the limitations we are experiencing.

Now let us look at the remainder of the houses more closely.

◆ House of Six-Metal

 This is a house where things move forward in your life. There is a sense of being in control of situations. Your past efforts pay off as things come together during this time. At the same time, the resulting harvest can lead you to be arrogant and cast an aura of entitlement. Thus you can be pushy, argumentative and self-righteous. You must learn the difference between manifesting your capabilities in a direct and forthright manner and just plain showing off.

Generally, your physical condition will be strong and active in this house, but there are precautions to take. Be wary of accidents while in some form of transport. Moving accidents can lead to injuries to the head or nerves. Excess heat should be avoided. Watch closely any injuries to the chest region, the brain and the bones. On an emotional level, there may be a tendency to cling rigidly to ideas, even in the face of information that proves that they are inaccurate or inappropriate. The kind of pushy behaviour mentioned above may be symptomatic of that tendency.

The numbers 9, 4, and 3 should be especially mindful when occupying this house.

◆ House of Seven-Metal

 There is a sense of ease in this house. It is a time of fruition where what comes to one seemingly involves no effort. Yet what is taking place is not happenstance, but the direct result of previous effort. To think differently, kick back and act frivolously at this time is to risk losing as much as one stands to gain.

Thus the challenge of the times is to be wary of becoming intoxicated by good fortune, on a personal, material or financial level. Enjoy, but maintain balance. Sloppiness in action will lead to misunderstandings. You may find that artistic and aesthetic appreciation is heightened at this time, but this may lead you to be seduced by appearances. The handling of money and property (including possibilities and deals) needs more care. Attraction between men and women here may lead to affairs, but will not necessarily have any lasting value. It is a good time to be more mindful of assessing your circumstances and possibly creating a new order in your life.

People with the numbers, 4, 3 and 9 will find this house challenging. Generally, those visiting this house should be mindful of injuries to the mouth, respiratory tract and bone fractures resulting from accidents. On an emotional level, there is a tendency to lose focus and become caught up in romantic notions not grounded in reality.

◆ House of Eight-Earth

 This is a house of inner depth. Stillness is the sign of the times. A person whose natal numbers are in the house may feel bogged down, and may therefore project a lot, appearing pushy and obstinate. The reason may be that they want to see things happen around them, because little may be happening for them personally. Others may find the person uncharacteristically cool or reserved.

Rather than fight the stillness, it is best to go with the energetics of the times and to be willing to look deep and honestly within yourself. If you do this you will be able to look into depths perhaps previously unnoticed or difficult to tap. For those whose numbers control or are controlled by eight-earth (1, 3 and 4), there may arise a keener sense of stagnation, frustration or hopelessness as they enter and occupy this house. A change of direction may occur as old patterns are looked at with more honesty. Ceremony will give way to sincerity.

Circulatory, joint and bone problems may arise at this time. Moreover, other people may inflict injuries on you because they don't understand your internal quietness and uncharacteristic stubbornness.

◆ House of Nine-Fire

Fire lights things up. It reveals. Consequently, this is a time of fame and fortune, where what you have done receives public attention. It may also be that what you wish to conceal is also revealed. Thus it can be a time of embarrassment to those whose dealings with others, with society or with the law, may be less than honest. Criminal proceedings may occur at this time.

On a personal level, you may find that a new sphere of friends and contacts arises while old ones disappear. Some of these changes are a natural progression. Some may lead you not to treat seriously or with care the connections and friends you already have. Thus discernment is advised and flamboyance is to be guarded against.

Water (one) and metal/air (six, seven) people will especially feel the 'heat' and must watch, more carefully than others whose numbers enter this house, for illnesses arising from fire energetics. Fevers, burns, irritation of the eyes, circulatory problems and epidemic-type illnesses need to be guarded against.

There is a general sense of lightness at this time which may become ungrounded. Loss of balance may give rise to hysteria or anxiety. A fire can only remain alight if one is prudent with fuel. Beware of over-extending yourself.

◆ House of One-Water

This is the house of winter and the north. It is a dark period where there is little movement on the surface. Caution is needed during these times and excessive activity can result in accidents and rapid dissipation of energy. When visiting this house, it is best to be quiet and reflective. Meditation, time for personal reflection, research into the deeper matters of life, will create a stronger knowledge base from which to act. Finances may be difficult at these times and one must be conservative with outlays. This is not a time to be innovative. Wait until you move out of this house before embarking on new ideas and ventures. There may be unexpected expenses.

On a personal level, you may find that friends and associates appear to keep their distance. This is because, when you are experiencing the House of One, you are less expressive, probably more enigmatic, and thus leave people feeling somewhat uncertain of their relationship to you. There is nevertheless a strong intuitive sense operating at these times, and thus the nuances of relationships are seen more clearly. If stress arises, this intuition may become hypersensitivity, in which case a person in this house may develop some fear, even paranoia, about getting close to others.

Illnesses that have to do with fluids of the body – blood, lymph, water, semen – and their associated organs should be guarded against with appropriate preventive measures. It is also best to be wary of hazards from liquids in the environment, like poor-quality water, overconsumption of alcohol, floods or toxic waste. The numbers 9, 2 and 5 should be particularly mindful at these times.

◆ House of Two-Earth

This is a time when not much of significance happens, and any efforts to make things happen will usually result in negative outcomes and reactions from others. You can stick to the mundane with moderate success at such times. However, with greater plans or ideas, you should accumulate rather than initiate. You can accumulate money, resources, allies, etc. in preparation for a new venture, but don't start just yet.

Beware of excessive banter and boasting about what you can do. During this time people occupying this house may appear uncharacteristically superficial. This could put off needed allies.

On an emotional level, a person whose natal numbers are in this house may experience a general state of worry that pervades many areas of their life. They may also find themselves over-involved in the concerns of others. As regards health, physical problems with lymphatics and other aspects of the earth element need to be guarded against. People with natal numbers 1, 3 and 4 should be generally more conscious of these effects when in the House of Two.

◆ House of Three-Tree/Space

This house possesses the power and energy of spring. Ideas come flooding in and with them the energy to begin undertakings of grand proportions. In this house, people find their creativity stimulated. However, there can be an accompanying lack of groundedness. Because the mind is so active, small but necessary details in projects may be overlooked. Consequently, although great things are possible, so are dismal failures.

When a person's natal numbers visit this house, there is a desire to get on and do things. If stifled or thwarted, frustration may ensue with a greater likelihood of outbursts of anger. Even the calmest person may find themselves breaking out at this time, and vocal expression tends to be louder and more direct than usual. Physical activity and expression increase.

Because of this increased expression, there may be an imbalance involving the nervous system and tree/space-related organs and tissues (such as the liver, gall bladder, muscles and connective tissue) if preventive measures are not taken. You should remain physically active, watch your consumption of oil, flour products and animal food, and guard against exposure to easterly winds. Earth (2, 5, 8) and metal air (6, 7) people should be particularly mindful.

◆ House of Four-Tree/Space

This is a time when one sees tangible results in what one has previously initiated. Most affairs and dealings in your life will go smoothly. Because of this, you can focus more, become more contemplative, and act when the timing makes action appropriate. There is, however, the tree/space tendency towards impetuosity. You should guard against this as it is unnecessary and may, in fact, undermine possible accomplishments, rather like pulling a plant out of the ground to see how it is growing. Using the vision of tree/space energy, one can steer things in the best direction. Thus the formula for getting things done should be look, think, then act.

Communication skills are enhanced at this time and the use of voice and media can be quite effective. Just don't lead people on.

There is a natural maturity of outlook here, and anything to the contrary has more to do with self-sabotage and confusion than with outside influences.

Imbalances that may arise during this time are paralysis and digestive and respiratory tract ailments. You should be mindful of the same aspects of lifestyle as mentioned in the description of the House of Three-Tree/Space, paying particular attention to keeping the throat and chest warm and away from draughts. Earth (2, 5, 8) and metal/air (6, 7) people are more susceptible to the imbalances inherent in this house.

The Adult and Child Numbers Together

Broadly speaking, the adult natal year number expresses itself as positive potential. Traits of growth and self-actualization in the physical, mental and spiritual dimensions of our lives are associated with this number. If such traits or potentials are not visible or expressed in a person's way of being, it is likely that there is either a self-limiting factor or some outside influence impinging on them. This would also account for any imbalances or illness associated with the particular natal year number.

The child natal month number also expresses potentials, but because it is by nature more dependent on environment and circumstances than the natal year, there is a greater tendency to weaknesses, imbalances and general stress symptoms. It may be that a person is living out of their natal month number experience in terms of relationships, jobs, preferences and responsibilities. They may function well in all these circumstances and arenas, but not without risking a greater tendency to stress and related imbalances in their lives.

This does not imply that the child number influence is to be ignored and only the natal year number enhanced. In fact, where the natal month number shows its greatest usefulness is in the way we learn to promote self-nurturing. Direction and action are best served by living from the natal year experience while nurturing is best served by understanding the interaction between both the child month and the adult year natal number energetics. It is important to understand this interaction if you truly want to create a life that is balanced, meaningful and satisfying.

Like the general guidelines presented for the transformation interactions that occur when the child natal month number resides in a certain house, there are similar guidelines for the transformation interactions between child and adult natal numbers. These guidelines are useful irrespective of the more particular elemental mix. Of course, for deeper insights the reader is advised to study the various dimensions of Five Transformations Theory.

Muramoto's book *Healing Ourselves* is once again recommended for those wishing to study these concepts further, as are the Nine Star Ki books by Takashi Yoshikawa and Michio Kushi listed in the Bibliography. A unique aspect of *The Complete Guide to Nine Star Ki*, however, is that the dimensions of Nine Star Ki that we are discussing at present are more thoroughly presented here than in any other book the author has been able to find.

Once again it is the mother–son and ko cycle principles within the Law of Five Transformations that are at work here. (See Figures 12 and 13.) The key words in the descriptions that follow are *support*, *control* and *same as*. The child natal number can support the adult natal number (e.g. 9(3)) or vice versa (e.g. 3(9)). (Note that the adult natal number is always *outside* the parentheses and the child number *inside* them.) The child number can also control the adult number (4(7)) or vice versa (7(4)). There are also combinations in which the transformations of the child and adult natal numbers are the same (e.g. 2(8)). If the two numbers are identical (4(4), 2(2) etc.), the previous chapter shows how they both reside in and are impacted by the House of Five (see page 107).

To discover which description fits the birth-date you have chosen to look at, you can either scan the descriptions below for the number combination you are looking for or refer to the Easy Reference Table (Figure 10, page 25). However, as you become more familiar with the Law of Five Transformations, you will be able to find the most relevant descriptions relatively easily.

When the child natal number transformation supports the adult natal number transformation: 9(3), 9(4), 2(9), 5(9), 8(9), 6(2), 6(5), 6(8), 7(2), 7(5), 7(8), 1(6), 1(7), 3(1), 4(1)

In this situation, there is a natural transition from childhood to adulthood. The child, in the mother position of the mother–son law of acupuncture theory, nurtures the adult transformation; thus the person does not have a sense of trauma about what life offers them. Even as an adult, the child qualities exhibited or indulged in usually help to enhance the adult expression. Consequently, even the stresses and imbalances that arise from the child natal month transformation are taken in their stride and the lessons to be learned from such experiences are more fully integrated than in any of the other child-adult configurations.

When the adult natal number transformation supports the child natal number transformation: 3(9), 4(9), 9(2), 9(5), 9(8), 2(6) 2(7), 5(6), 5(7), 8(6), 8(7), 6(1), 7(1), 1(3), 1(4)

As in the previous description, there is a sense of ease or compatibility between adult and child experience. In the previous example, the child was supportive of the adult. Here it is the other way round. Thus a person with this configuration may find that they are expressing their natal year potential when suddenly their more child natal month patterns begin to emerge into interactions. They may as a result become demanding or pushy in situations in which they originally had a clearer perspective. In such circumstances, some form of supportive confrontation is usually needed to bring the person to their senses; this can be from within themselves or from someone else. In either case, there is not much tension or strain involved in re-establishing a more balanced and harmonious interaction.

When the adult natal number transformation controls the child natal number transformation: 3(2), 3(5), 3(8), 4(2), 4(8), 9(6), 9(7), 2(1), 5(1), 8(1), 6(3), 6(4), 7(3), 7(4), 1(9)

Here is a situation where the person exhibits a tremendous amount of self-control. Like a superego, the adult natal transformation acts as a reminder to the child natal transformation of a higher order of things – not literally higher, but in the sense of being looked at by oneself from a different, more independent perspective. This may curb impulsiveness but it can also result in a person overlooking or considering unimportant many childhood nurturing needs. Thus they may be highly self-repressive and are often loners.

At an early age, they may be considered good children as their self-monitoring keeps them in line. They tend to be rather self-critical and are better at admonishing themselves than anyone else in their lives could be. Unless their parents possess an adult or child number that is the same as their adult natal number, they will have little impact in disciplining them. In fact, if they are admonished by someone else, it is almost as if insult has been added to injury. They usually know when they are out of line.

Such a number configuration could lead to problems in situations where there is a hierarchy or authority structure to be related to. Two opposing tendencies could arise: total compliance or total defiance.

When the child natal number transformation controls the adult natal number transformation: 2(3), 2(4), 5(3), 5(4), 8(3), 8(4), 1(2), 1(5), 1(8), 9(1), 6(9), 7(9), 3(6), 3(7), 4(6), 4(7)

In such configurations, there is a tendency towards impetuous behaviour. Here is a situation where a person's adult potentials and their ability to deal with situations are constantly being challenged by childhood patterns and responses. Independence and assertiveness are challenged by constant reminders of their limitations, conditions and habitual patterns. A person may thus give up their ideals, procrastinate, abdicate responsibility or blame others. There is a resulting tendency towards conscious or unconscious manipulation in relationships with others.

In such a situation, you should try to determine what the actual nurturing needs of the child natal month expression are. By acknowledging these needs and trying to meet them, you can lighten the pressures or control on the adult number transformation, thus allowing the adult expression to arise more freely.

When the child and adult natal numbers share the same transformation but are different in their number: 2(5), 2(8), 3(4), 4(3), 5(2), 5(8), 6(7), 7(6), 8(2), 8(5)

Many of the characteristics of the same adult and child number, as explained in the previous chapter, apply here. However, because there is a numerical variation, the yin and yang aspects are also represented. Thus the person has greater physical resilience and emotional perspective and flexibility than the double-numbered person – that is, a person whose adult natal year and child natal month numbers are the same. The personality is more well rounded from the standpoint of one transformation. In a sense, such people could be considered archetypes of the transformation that their numbers represent. They can thus exude a confidence not seen in double-numbered combinations.

◆ Gender energetics and the adult/child configuration

As stated previously, in the cycle of nine numbers, there are those with a more contractive nature and those with a more expansive nature. This applies in the annual, monthly and daily cycles. Throughout Oriental thought, contractive and expansive qualities have been metaphorically referred to in gender terms. The more yang or contractive numbers are thus referred to as being masculine in nature, while the more yin or expansive numbers are referred to as being feminine in nature. In Nine Star Ki, 2, 4, 7 and 9 are considered feminine, while 1, 3, 6 and 8 are considered masculine. The number 5 is considered either masculine or feminine. (In the work of Rex Lassalle, the number 5 is ascribed the gender of the person concerned, as well as the attributes of a two-earth if the person is female, or eight-earth if the person is male. At the same time, it is my experience that while this is true, one will also find that the person will exhibit opposite gender and earth number tendencies as well as tendencies distinctive to five-earth natal energetics. Thus when a five is a part of a person's Nine Star Ki chart, it is important to examine two-, five- and eight-earth characteristics as well as masculine and feminine tendencies and the various gender energetic configurations as described below.)

For example, for a person born on 13 April 1946, the natal year number is 9 and the month is 3. The configuration would be written as 9(3) eight. If we take into consideration the gender of the natal year and month numbers, the same configuration would be written as 9*f*(3*m*) eight*m*, *f* standing for female and *m* for male.

Although the gender typology would not change for the

numbers, Gagne and Mann, in their *Nine Ki Handbook,* note that the impact of the gender of the numbers does differ depending on whether the person is male or female. In the example given above, if the person being considered is female, then the female attribute of 9 is considered the same as her gender, whereas the male aspect of 3 is considered opposite to her gender. If the person were male, the opposite would be the case; 9 would be opposite his gender, while 3 would be the same. When 5 is either the adult or the child number, it should be considered both masculine and feminine at the start. One can then look at the masculine–feminine configurations to see which is best suited to the character of the person being evaluated.

For example, let us assume John is a 6 natal year with a 5 natal month. Six is masculine and 5 can be either feminine or masculine. Thus John's gender energetic configuration could be male–female or male–male. In the typology being used, this would make John a same–opposite or same–same. John would therefore read the material for both to see which one he identifies with most. And, because of the extreme nature of the number 5, it could also be that in some circumstances he feels one way and in others he feels the other way.

Gagne and Mann use this 'same' and 'opposite' concept in the development of their four basic gender configurations: same/same, same/opposite, opposite/same and opposite/opposite. Especially in relation to other people, the configuration of the gender energetics can have a noted impact. Because Gagne and Mann's method of presenting these configurations works so well. I have – with thanks to Stephen Gagne – elected to keep to their format. A brief description of each configuration follows.

When looking at these descriptions it is important to view genders from a polarity rather than a dualistic, either/or, perspective. The fact of the matter is that we embody both. The dominance of the force of one gender at the time of birth (as yin and yang are never equal) leads to the formation and experience of the particular gender that we are. At the same time, to become a 'whole' person, we must learn to integrate the male and female aspects of our being.

SAME/SAME: *Males that are* 1(1), 1(3), 1(6), 1(8), 3(1), 3(3), 3(6), 3(8), 6(1), 6(3), 6(6), 6(8), 8(1), 8(3), 8(6), 8(8). *Females that are* 2(2), 2(4), 2(7), 2(9), 4(2), 4(4), 4(7), 4(9), 7(2), 7(4), 7(7), 7(9), 9(2), 9(4), 9(7), 9(9)

> These are people that are confident in their gender identity and expression. Consequently, they rarely have any conflict within themselves as regards self-expression. They relate easily with both males and females.
>
> Because they are strongly influenced by their own gender ener-getics, they often find it difficult to empathize with the opposite sex. They will also idealize the opposite sex, and people of the opposite sex may have difficulty living up to the same/same's expectations. As they expect a relationship to go the way they want it to, they do not catch on quickly when relationships are going awry. Thus they may hold on to relationships and go on in dysfunctional ways longer than is useful to either partner. If they are not in a long-standing relationship, they may have several casual relationships (either in sequence or at once) while waiting for their ideal to appear. At the same time, they may remain aloof. In terms of sexual activity, they can remain abstinent for long periods (and thus easily adapt to a monastic life) or just enjoy sexuality in a more playful way.
>
> These people rarely have problems with their reproductive systems. Their sexual potency is strong.

SAME/OPPOSITE: *Males that are* 1(2), 1(4), 1(7), 1(9), 3(2), 3(4), 3(7), 3(9), 6(2), 6(4), 6(7), 6(9), 8(2), 8(4), 8(7), 8(9). *Females that are* 2(1), 2(3), 2(6), 2(8), 4(1), 4(3), 4(6), 4(8), 7(1), 7(3), 7(6), 7(8), 9(1), 9(3), 9(6), 9(8)

> These people have their own gender in the natal year position and the opposite gender in the natal month position. This configu-ration gives them a positive self-image. They have the confidence and depth of their own gender in their self-expressive aspect (natal year) and a direct experience of the opposite polarity or gender in their conditional aspect. As they are in touch with both aspects of their being in a way that evokes ease in their being, they can usually empathize with both men and women. Such people make excellent counsellors and confidants to the opposite sex, who

usually find it easy to relate to the same/opposite. Same/opposites may even prefer to have more friends of the opposite sex, which may arouse jealousy and concern in their own partners or the partners of their friends. However, they are rarely flirtatious – just more relaxed around the opposite sex.

Under stress, same/opposites may find that their generally relaxed manner gives way to a sense of unease and insecurity. Self-doubt and gender insecurity can lead to periods of emotional (and sexual) repression or misgivings.

OPPOSITE/SAME: *Males that are* 2(1), 2(3), 2(6), 2(8), 4(1), 4(3), 4(6), 4(8), 7(1), 7(3), 7(6), 7(8), 9(1), 9(3), 9(6), 9(8). *Females that are* 1(2), 1(4), 1(7), 1(9), 3(2), 3(4), 3(7), 3(9), 6(2), 6(4), 6(7), 6(9), 8(2), 8(4), 8(7), 8(9)

These people are somewhat self-conscious of their gender identity. They tend to act characteristically masculine or feminine in accordance with stereotypes and images. However, when challenged, they become confronted with a basic insecurity and can experience much self-doubt.

Because their adult natal number is opposite to their own gender, the opposite/same has a deep understanding of the opposite sex. They can be excellent at objectively viewing another person's situation or predicament. However, they easily get caught up in their own feelings, the stereotypes and the social standards around them. They long for deep relationships and must come to terms with the fact that when they do not find them, it has more to do with their own inner tensions than the inadequacies of others. Also, the bravado with which they act in times of self-doubt can be a factor that inhibits authentic contact with others.

OPPOSITE/OPPOSITE: *Males that are* 2(2), 2(4), 2(7), 2(9), 4(2), 4(4), 4(7), 4(9), 7(2), 7(4), 7(7), 7(9), 9(2), 9(4), 9(7), 9(9). *Females that are* 1(1), 1(3), 1(6), 1(8), 3(1), 3(3), 3(6), 3(8), 6(1), 6(3), 6(6), 6(8), 8(1), 8(3), 8(6), 8(8)

These are people who lack the strength of their own gender energetics. Because of this, there is a certain level of constant discomfort in their being. Life always seems a challenge to an opposite/opposite. There is a sense of struggle about life and what it offers. Thus these people are usually extremely wilful. They get on and do things and project a confidence which comes from their constant feeling that they have to keep their chin up and push on in life.

Because their gender identity is based on the strength of the opposite gender energetic, the opposite sex plays the role of antagonist in their lives. Because of their personal sense of command, the opposite/opposite may create a persona which is alluring, intense and possibly confusing to those attracted to them. What often happens in this situation and in others where the opposite/opposite has dealings with the opposite sex, is that they may create tensions, misunderstandings and conflict. In an attempt to temper the strength of the opposite gender in their personality, the opposite/opposite may project outward and see all faults and sources of aggravation as arising from the opposite sex. (From a psychoanalytical point of view, it may even be that this projection creates a feeling of lack of support from the parent opposite their own gender – daughter to father, son to mother – thus creating a state of mind in later life where detachment from parental influences or images becomes problematic.) They tend to belittle or exploit the opposite sex in personal relationships. This accounts for a tendency to go to extremes in sexual relationships where they can be either resolutely abstinent or totally hedonistic. The experience of sex can play an inordinately important role as a reference point in a relationship, yet at the same time, be devoid of any personal experience of pleasure or satisfaction. On a physical level, the opposite/opposite energetic can lead to chronic or continuous imbalances and disease of the reproductive tract.

Such people usually find that they can relax more in the presence of their own gender. As they look to role models of their own gender they may also idealize the lives of those they look up to or wish to emulate. With all the discomfort and inner tension they may experience, the opposite/opposite's 'life-as-a-challenge' mentality makes them exceedingly hard working and dedicated to whatever causes, endeavours or missions they set their minds to. Thus they are an inspiration to those around them. As such they often become leaders with devoted followers.

The Dynamics of Relationships

When one looks at relationships in the context of the I Ching, the medical system of acupuncture and the laws of nature as conceived in the Law of Five Transformations, one is addressing our basic inter-connectedness with the world.

In the realm of personal and professional relationships, therefore, there is no judgement on any relationship – it is not good or bad. It is just a matter of understanding how elements or transformations interact. Some interactions flow; others create challenges, blockages etc. To say that one situation or interaction is better than another is to miss the point. Relationships do not need to be serene to be meaningful and a source of support and growth for the persons concerned. In fact, as the transformations are stimulated and activated in accordance with the seasons, the years and changing circumstances, one will not find a relationship which can be defined in one given way as if static.

In no way does such a statement contradict the notion that there are fundamental energetic interactions which do persist over time. By analogy, an apple is an apple all the time. However, there are phases in the life of an apple that are harder and softer, sweeter and more sour, etc. Thus, while seeing that we have an apple in front of us, the qualities of that apple will vary according to where it is in its life cycle. Indeed, our relationship to the apple will vary depending on what our preferences are and the state of the apple. Relationships between humans are no different, and they need to be viewed dynamically. Viewed dynamically, the way in which we relate changes in accordance with what aspects of ourselves are being activated at any given time as a result of circumstances, both internal and external. From this point of view, one can say that all relationships are workable. What makes them unworkable is our fixation with outcomes.

Four points need to be made with regard to the way in which a relationship can be facilitated. First, what makes a relationship workable is our willingness to face ourselves and be true to who we are. Secondly, when we do this we come to realize that all beings are striving for the same things we strive for and that, thirdly, there are differences of approach, according to personal strengths, weaknesses and circumstances. Lastly all relationships die in the wake of assumptions made by the partners, and any relationship can survive, flourish and thrive in an atmosphere of openness, humour and love.

Nine Star Ki is invaluable in helping us to get in touch with our basic, conditioned nature with all its strengths and weaknesses. With a self-assessment that is based on elemental/transformational factors rather than cultural stereotypes or ideals we can more creatively and accurately develop our skills and potentials. Becoming more honest and familiar with ourselves on such a level, we learn to relax with who we are. We learn to become friends with ourselves. This is, in fact, the first and necessary step towards being able to extend friendship to others and relate in an authentic way.

Knowing ourselves better in a positive way, we next need to be able to appreciate and relate to others as they are. Generally, one needs an attitude of openness, humour and love, as mentioned above. In themselves, these three can help to cut through almost any situation. At the same time, often because of our perceptions and projections, our relationships can remain bogged down in confusion with the resulting misunderstandings. In such situations, the Ki can be a way of tapping into how such confusion and misunderstanding arise by examining the general qualities, in particular the psychological predispositions inherent in the various transformations dominant in the make-up of the persons concerned.

Up until this point, we have been addressing the elemental/transformational mixes that create styles of relating for any individual. It is now time to demonstrate how this same model can be used to analyse styles of interaction between individuals.

◆ Perception

It is commonly recognized in various schools of psychology that our view of the world is based on our experience of it. It is also becoming increasingly clear in psychology that the events in our lives are not meaningful in themselves. What gives them meaning is our perceptions, reactions and responses, which build upon each other, layer after layer. Much of the material presented thus far has been about ways in which each transformation phase influences our perceptions, reactions and responses. It has also been stressed how the natal year and natal month transformations form a constitutional core from which our world is experienced.

We are born with a particular natal adult year and natal child month. In the year we are born, our natal year number occupies the House of Five and our natal month occupies whichever house it reaches in the movement of numbers through time and space. This is not only true of our own numbers. It also means that all numbers are in a particular position based on the given year. Except in a five-earth year, the numbers do not occupy their own houses. Thus each number's transformation will possess qualities based on the house it occupies.

On an interpersonal level, this means that when we encounter someone, the transformations that make up the natal adult and child characteristics of that person reside in certain houses in our natal chart. This is how we will experience their transformations. Briefly stated, we see their qualities through our filters.

Depending on our own personal balance and sensitivity, we may be able to distinguish what is truly them and what is just our perceptual framework. However, it is not uncommon for us to blur the two. In Nine Star Ki terms, this means mistaking the transformation qualities of the other person for the house qualities and the interactions between the transformation and the houses that we experience. An example will quickly clarify this concept and how it impacts on our perceptions and relationships.

Let us look at a three-tree/space year.

In a three-tree/space year, one-water sits in the House of Three-

Tree. A three-tree person encountering a one-water person generally finds them supportive, as water is the mother of tree/space. However, the internal perception of the three-tree person will go further than that. For the three-tree, the one-water person sits in the tree house of ideas, inspiration and new energy. Thus the three-tree person may find that they are nourished with these qualities by the one-water person.

This is fine in itself. It gets distorted, however, when the three-tree person expects the one-water person to interact and respond in accordance with the energetics of the House of Three. The three-tree may not see the cautiousness and reflection that has gone into the ideas the one-water presents to them. Thus they may overlook the one-water's reserved nature and expect bouncing enthusiasm. With such a distortion communications with the one-water may become stifling. Inner perception here is not congruent with outer reality.

We can all fall prey to such a way of viewing others. The issue here is not that it is wrong. Rather we must learn to distinguish between what the basic energetic patterns of the other person are and what their energetics become when viewed from our particular frame of reference. It is a useful self-reflective process to observe how our own energetics change on a month-by-month basis, depending on what houses our own natal numbers reside in. As we come to be more sensitive to this within ourselves, it becomes easier to see others more clearly. If nothing else, it relaxes our tendency towards fixation.

Figure 14. Universal Chart for a three-tree/space year.

◆ Interacting

If we relate to our world only on the basis of our inner perceptions, in other words our filters, we are in for a rude awakening.
In some ways the inner perceptions view is useful in so far as it
shows us how we take in our world. In extending back out into
the world by communicating, a change of focus is needed.

It seems quite evident these days that communications between
individuals, couples, groups and nations are rife with problems.
These problems may simply stem from the fact that we are re-
sponding to the world only from the standpoint of our perceptions of our needs and assuming that everything and everyone else
operates in the same way.

Being who we are, our relationship to the world is based on our
own natal year numbers being in the centre of the Magic Square.
This being the case, it is almost as if all inner perceptions are
cancelled. As everyone in a relationship is speaking from their
centre (with their natal year number at the centre), it is almost as if
no one is in the centre. Relating creates balance. We have to get
out of our heads and relate to what is in front of us. If we don't,
misunderstanding is inevitable.

On a practical level, what this means is that the standard Five
Transformation chart is the best way to identify what the actual
elemental energetics are in a relationship. The Magic Square and
its houses can thus be simplified as in Figure 15.

Once set in this standard configuration, one can plot the natal
month and year numbers of each individual within a particular
interaction with the given transformations. From this, the responses and reactions that occur in the course of the relationship
can be examined based on transformation energetics. Of course
there are the house influences and monthly and yearly variations
to be taken into account. However, the configuration of energetics as presented on the basic Five Transformation chart will be
the underlying core dynamic in the relationship.

◆ Taking a Couple as an Example

What we shall now do is look at a relationship. The steps suggested in the example will be the ones you can take to look at any
relationship.

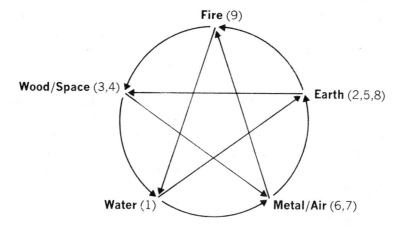

Figure 15. The standard Five Transformation chart showing elemental energetics in a relationship.

John was born on 18 March 1947 and his wife, Jennifer, was born on 6 August 1953. They come to a Nine Star Ki counsellor wanting to gain more insight into their relationship. To do this, the following method is recommended.

First, study the information pertaining to your own natal year adult and natal month child numbers. Note the adult potentials and the potential and stress patterns of the natal month number. Read the material about transformation combinations and gender energetics.

In John's case, 18 March 1947 makes him a 8m(1m) seven*f*. He should see that he is a deep thinker, strong in masculine character, and not very expressive emotionally. He likes to take his time deliberating over matters and is a hard worker. He may be too serious and may often find himself taking things too literally. As earth (eight) is his adult and controls water (one) as his child, John is rather self-controlled and self-critical, he does not take criticism from others well. His more fluid child side is suppressed in many areas and thus will exhibit one-water stress-related problems. He may at times seem withdrawn and depressed. Initial signs of stress may be the result of trying to please people or having fears which he tries to mask so as not to upset those around him. Although a generally caring man, his masculine/masculine, hence same/same gender energetics can sometimes make him naïve, or oblivious to the needs of women. He may even idealize the women in his life, not recognizing how this can set them and him up for disappointment or failure.

In Jennifer's case, 6 August 1953 makes her a 2f(6m) ninef. Briefly, Jennifer has both primal mother (two-earth) and primal father (six-metal) characteristics. A generally caring individual, Jennifer may find that she is other people's confidant, and involved excessively in their lives. Her two-earth nature makes her very sympathetic. Yet because earth is the mother of metal (and her six), Jennifer may find that she leaps from concern to judgements and actions in other people's lives before the time is appropriate. She may even be rather argumentative in such circumstances, pushing her point a bit too far. However, as people see her as a responsible person, they may allow her to take over, abdicating their own responsibility. Thus, Jennifer may tend to burn herself out.

Stress for her may manifest as anxiety which then precipitates rigid stubbornness or a sense of hysteria that is somewhat ill-focused. There are many 'shoulds' in her life. Her female/male or same/opposite gender energetics generally allow her to feel at ease in herself and she can relate well to either sex. This ease, together with her socializing ways may make others see her as flirtatious, perhaps superficial. As a result she may find that partners are jealous and covetous.

Second, after this brief character evaluation, plot the natal year and month numbers of the other person in the relationship on your chart, that is, with your natal year in the House of Five. Simply put, with your natal year number in the centre, you are looking at the houses in which the other person's number resides. This will give you your inner perception or experience of the other person on transformation and house level.

Let's look at John's chart in Figure 16 to see where Jennifer fits in.

Jennifer's two-earth adult sits in John's House of eight, while her six-metal child sits in the House of three. This means that John sees Jennifer in her adult nature as someone with whom he probably sees eye to eye. Because the two-earth which is softer in

7	3	5
6	8	1
2	4	9

Figure 16. John's chart

its quality occupies the House of Eight, John may overlook Jennifer's softer nature. He may expect her to be stoical and hardworking, someone who drives herself as hard as she can. He may also look to Jennifer as someone to sort out details and perhaps when he is bogged down, to pull him up. Being emotionally unexpressive, John may find it difficult to understand when Jennifer is emotional. Also, Jennifer's six-metal sits in John's House of Three. As tree controls earth, John may experience Jennifer as coming up with lots of ideas, but those ideas, although pragmatic and seemingly logical, may challenge or threaten him and his plans.

Now let's look at Jennifer's chart to see where John fits in.

1	6	8
9	2	4
5	7	3

Figure 17. Jennifer's chart

John's eight-earth adult sits in Jennifer's House of Two while his one-water child sits in the House of Four. Here we have a situation where John and Jennifer's internal perceptions almost match, thus possibly creating many expectations and assumptions. John's eight-earth in the House of Two leads Jennifer to feel that both she and John see the world in the same way. However, Jennifer, being more expressive, may be confused by John's lack of expression and the way he gets caught up in situations and considers things that Jennifer sees as trifling. She may ask, 'Why he is taking things so seriously?'

Jennifer finds John very caring, but may expect him to be more malleable and expressive than he is capable of being. At the same time, John's one-water is in her House of Four. Thus John may come up with ideas for Jennifer that are both well thought out and meaningful, but at the same time, challenge Jennifer's two-earth nature and irritate her need for control and for feeling responsible (six-metal aspect). She may nevertheless look to John for creativity and inspiration, and view his lack of expressiveness as a way of concealing things from her. She may even think that he is basically angry with her or that when he doesn't say what is on his mind, it is an act of hostility.

Third, use the standard Five Transformation chart to plot both numbers. Use lower case letters to indicate the child transformation and capitals to indicate the adult transformation. Place the number beside the name in each case. Such a chart will give you the actual basic energetics occurring during interaction.

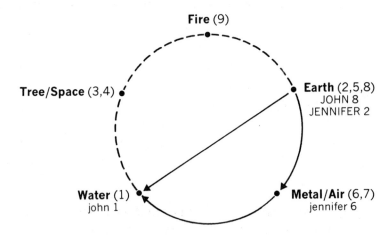

Figure 18. The standard Five Transformation chart for John and Jennifer.

Based on such a map one can make the following observations of John and Jennifer's interactions.

Both John and Jennifer have their adult numbers in the earth transformation, indicating that they see eye to eye in many ways and that the yin (two) of Jennifer and yang (eight) of John create enough of a difference in expression to make their relationship dynamic. (If both were eight or two, although there would be much in common, there might also be a sense of stagnation in the relationship, as if nothing is moving forward. *This can be true of any relationship where the numbers of the respective partners are the same.*) Both John and Jennifer like to get on and do things,

In general, Jennifer feels more supported by John than vice versa. Here John's eight-earth adult is the mother element to Jennifer's six-metal child. Jennifer's two-earth is also the mother to her six-metal child. The result may be that as Jennifer has a natural tendency to slip into her six-metal child anyway, such a pattern is reinforced by John as well. Thus within the relationship, Jennifer may act more out of her child than her adult transformation. Six being the primal father number, she may find herself taking on too many responsibilities, being somewhat confrontational or argumentative, and being more concerned about the relationship than John appears to be. As this six-metal is reinforced by both John's 8 and Jennifer's 2, the dominance of six-metal in the relationship may encourage more one-water responses from John. Thus while eights are generally reserved in their communication, John may be even more cautious and uncommunicative as Jennifer's six-metal dominates interactions. John may even appear enigmatic as he feels less inclined to communicate directly what is on his mind. This may further upset Jennifer as she expects things to be on the surface and 'up front'.

Another dominant scenario in their interactions is that John is rather self-critical and controls his own behaviour (adult eight-earth controlling child one-water), so John may also feel Jennifer is being rather critical of him as her two-earth also controls one-water. Thus there are times when John almost feels emotionally set up by Jennifer; the mother–son relationship of John and Jennifer's numbers precipitates their child patterns, yet when activated into his one-water child response patterns, Jennifer's adult two-earth response can add insult to injury as John is already trying to get a grip on himself emotionally.

John's own self-doubt will be compounded by Jennifer's smothering and controlling tendencies. Whereas she may wish to act to clear the air, to a large extent John just wants to be left alone to think about things in his own time. Because Jennifer's numbers are supportive of each other and because she trusts that John does care for her and is supportive of her, his lack of response at times may be seen as stubbornness or an unwillingness to share. In fact, even in the best of circumstances it takes John some time to get to the point. It's not that he doesn't feel things; indeed, he feels very deeply. If Jennifer can be patient, she will find that what John conveys to her has depth and can bring new levels of meaning to their relationship. From Jennifer, John can learn that letting people know what is going on strengthens relationships. His tendency to isolation and silence can only weaken a relationship over time.

◆ What is the Value of Such Information?

As I have often said in this volume, no situation is unworkable. However, we get it into our minds that when communication is awkward or situations run counter to expectations there must be something wrong and something, therefore, must be fixed. A couple like John and Jennifer may find themselves in counselling trying to change something which is nothing more than a basic transformation dynamic expressing itself in social and psychological arenas.

If the significance of these dynamics is realized, the more supportive aspects of their relations could be emphasized and a more humorous and spacious approach could be adopted when they see some of the more conflicting patterns emerging in stressful situations. Obviously this can be more difficult than we would like, simply because most of us take our lives rather seriously and have particular definitions of who we are and what our relationships should be like. However, if we can begin by taking into account basic energetics and the patterns they create we may be able to come up with creative ways to bridge the gap between reality and our desires. If our desires are devoid of any basic reality, then we shall always pursue a self-identity and lasting meaningful relationships in vain.

As we accept reality, life becomes less and less of a problem. Drama gives way to relative *dharma* or truth.

◆ Application in Work and Business

In the realm of personal relationships and family matters, the usefulness of Nine Star Ki can be seen in the example of John and Jennifer. But how might it apply in other relationships, such as in the workplace? For it is a fact of most adults' experience that most of their waking hours are spent at work.

In 1985 and 1986, a good friend, Rex Lassalle, and I were doing some work and training with a Kentucky-based accounting firm. One of the sidelines of this firm was a computerized personality testing and evaluation service for employers looking for employees who would fit into their corporate settings. Over the years, technology in this field has become so precise in determining psychological and social make-up and character that not only are more firms relying on such testing but there have been fewer lawsuits by state and federal boards investigating discrimination when such tests are used compared to personal interviews by company personnel departments. It seems that such testing is more objective and accurate in creating the right employer–employee task mix.

Although effective, many of those tests are quite time-consuming to administer and costly to evaluate. The firm in this situation was using two separate systems. Mr Lassalle and I offered the use of Nine Star Ki at no cost, to see if the ki could pick up the same information just by having access to the prospective employees' birth-dates.

While we were not surprised at the results, the head of the firm was. The ki *can* be used to look at the numerous variables that employers want to know about; personalities, authority issues and likely responses, skills and general responses under stress. Looking at the profiles and descriptions found in this volume, such information is evident. Beyond this, however, the ki can also be used to determine how such an individual will interact with fellow workers.

The model presented for evaluating the relationship of our example couple is applicable here. The ki can be used to look at a new employee coming into an already existing system. This can be good news for personnel departments as it can not only be an effective evaluation tool, but also an exceedingly cost-effective one. But apart from new employees, all personnel departments are called upon to deal with morale and task issues of employee/ staff teams. Creating a Nine Star Ki map of all employees or working units is useful in that it can not only highlight all the individual strengths, weaknesses and potentials within a group, but also be used to determine routes of support, pockets of potential conflict, as well as the overall strengths, weaknesses and balance of an entire group at once. I have devised a systematic evaluation process that is useful for any group being studied.

This evaluation is broken down into four distinct phases in order to make data more coherent and usable for supervisors or team evaluators. Phase One involves questions a supervisor or evaluator should try to answer regarding individual team members. Phase Two is a chart where the adult and child natal numbers of each team member are plotted out under each of the nine numbers and their associated management or emphasized interaction skill. This chart will give supervisors or evaluators a visual picture of where the strengths, weaknesses and gaps in team functioning exist. At the bottom of the chart are management strategies that should be adopted to support, enhance or control various tendencies or individuals. Phase Three is an actual Five Transformation map with all the individuals plotted on it in their adult and child aspects. A narrative of group dynamics follows where each of the individuals in relation to others is highlighted. Phase Four is general comments and recommendations.

◆ Cardiovascular Lab Evaluated

The following example is a Nine-Star Ki evaluation of a cardiovascular lab of a large hospital system. The names used in the example are fictitious, but the birth-dates are actual ones. The people in this situation are not prospective but actual employees who have been working under the same supervisor for some time. The purpose of the evaluation here is thus to look at the individuals within and the operation of the entire team.

Please be aware that while the phases as they are presented and the language used in the discussion that follows regarding the cardiovascular lab will refer to 'supervisor' and 'employees', the participants can be members of a family, a counsellor looking at the dynamics of a therapy group, or any other group situation one

may want to look at from a Nine Star Ki perspective. The usefulness of giving the specific details of this group evaluation is that
they demonstrate Nine Star Ki's potential in identifying, clarifying and sorting out processes in group settings.

Phase One

In Phase One of an evaluation, a supervisor or evaluator needs to
ask the following four questions regarding members of the staff
team:

1. What are the employee's adult and child numbers and what
are the characteristics found within these numbers that best cor-
respond to the employee's job description? Attention should be
paid to the occupations as listed in the number profiles as well as
the general and business relationship narratives.

2. Of the management skills as listed in the profiles and the
relationship styles as described in the narrative of both adult and
child numbers, which are most in keeping with the employee's
job description, particularly in the area of interactions expected
with other employees?

3. From which number (child or adult) do you see the
employee operating generally?

4. What situations do you know of that bring out the
employee's adult traits? What situations bring out the employee's
child traits?

As we have already done basic character evaluations in our
description of John and Jennifer (see above), no descriptions of
the various employees is given here. You are advised when using
the system suggested to follow the questions in Phase One to get
the information you need to proceed to the other three phases.

Phase Two

In the mid-eighties, Warren Bellows and Nancy Post of the
Merriam Hill Centre in Cambridge, Massachusetts developed an
organization theory where types of managing and work skills
were classified as yin or yang aspects of one of the Five

Figure 19 (overleaf) Group Energetic Evaluation chart for the Merrian Hill Center

Number	1	2	3	4
Managing skills	**YIN – Allocator –** containing, storing, delineating boundaries, managing resources **YANG** - Motivator – generating, energizing, providing direction, reflection	**Supporter** sustaining, supporting, retaining, assimilating, anchoring, centring	**Planner** mapping, visioning, defining borders, strategizing, adapting, organizing	**Decision-Maker** clarifying, individuating, scheduling, initiating conflict, structuring
Persons involved	DAVE TANYA jim		JOHN DOROTHY dorothy JANE MIKE mike dave	DENISE
Strategy				
No. 1 Support for adult activation	**Metal/Air Action –** provide historical data, provide summations, get No. 1 to consider the broader social implications, provide space for reflection and response, fatherly support	**Fire Action –** be direct, be convincing, promote excitement, be joyful, overcome anxieties, demonstrate appreciation, find out what else they need, sell them the idea	**Water Action –** communicate general trends of situation, delineate boundaries for person, energize them to move in given direction, be a well-spring, gentle action with reserve	Same as 3 tree/space but appeal to their maturity and sense to see things clearly. Support in prioritizing
No. 2 Enhance to move person out of child activation	Strategy No. 1 followed by **Tree/ Space action –** be enthusiastic, show them what potential there is, let them know where things need to go, ask for their energy and gleanings from their reflections	Strategy No. 1 followed by **Metal/Air Action –** monitor quality, make them accountable, ask for progress reports, be accepting of what's offered, show social/ historical importance of work done	Strategy No. 1 followed by **Fire Action –** show them what is possible, weave them into a greater plan or network of people, be enthusiastic, clarify their ideas	Same as Strategy No. 1 for 3 tree/space, but make sure that encouragement allows them to stick to one direction and within time limits set
No. 3 Control inappropriate child action	**Earth Action –** ground them, listen to them. Get details from them regarding vague fears. Acknowledge but challenge hesitancy	**Tree/Space Action –** clarify person's situation, initiate conflict if necessary, restructure person's situation, define limits, prioritize	**Metal/Air Action –** make person accountable, spell it out, establish order in their activity, list consequences, refer to team commitment, social order, morality, avoid direct confrontation	Same as 3 tree/space in Strategy No. 3, but over-ride their muddledness. Overcome confusion by refining, giving a clear evaluation of the situation, bringing balance to their perspective

5	6	7	8	9
Consolidator catalysing, leading, sorting, critiquing, also traits for 2 and 8	**Inspirer** equilibrating, resonating, receiving, balancing, establishing order	**Evaluator** accounting, refining, eliminating, evolving, managing change, quality control	**Producer** nurturing, transporting, supporting, producing, attention to details, integrating	**YIN – Sorter –** selling, problem solving, discriminating, transforming and Networker – team building, socializing, atmosphere builder **YANG – Coordinator –** coordinating, defining roles, directing, cooperation-building, and **Communicator –** appreciating, creating trust, expressing protecting
john	denise tanya		jane	JIM
Fire Action – same as for 2 earth, but here over-ride indecisiveness, appeal to intellect, stimulate catalysing nature, define role, create trust, be supportive	**Earth Action –** nurture, provide adequate details, be an anchor, listen	Same as Strategy No. 1 for 6 metal, but more anchoring and centering, offer positive criticism, help to sustain momentum	Same as Strategy No. 1 for 2 and 5 earth, but help person to relax more, provide enthusiasm, lightness, and clarity, help with discrimination and priority	**Tree/Space Action –** provide ideas, give vision, enthusiasm and excitement, stimulate, map the territory to be explored, provide supportive muscle, create context
Same as Strategy No. 1 in 2 earth, followed by **Metal/Air Action –** critically weigh up options, help person adjust to change, establish order, encourage person to produce results, balance action	Strategy No. 1 followed by **Water Action –** reflect back, be receptive, manage resources, overcome rigidity by providing larger perspective	Strategy No. 1 followed by **Water Action –** as with 6 metal but here be more conservative, provide more direction, facilitate more truthful responses	Strategy No. 1 followed by **Metal/Air Action –** help to eliminate excess, refine, help person to focus beyond task, engage in play	Strategy No. 1 followed by **Earth Action –** get it all focused, encourage to act, spell out the end product, encourage diligence, provide realistic outlook and expectations, help person to match talk and actions
As Strategy No. 3 for 2 earth, getting person to commit themselves, over-ride sentimentality, encourage independence, provide time limits, give commands, help person to vision	**Fire Action –** spell it out, challenge dualistic (blank/white) thinking, overcome arrogance, clear air before grudges are set	**Fire Action –** don't buy smooth talk, challenge sense of entitlement, overcome any melancholy, keep person task-focused, appeal to social values and importance of the team	**Tree/Space Action –** snap person out of wallowing or hopelessness, encourage independent thinking, provide vision, even reframe structure, provide time frames	**Water Action –** listen, provide reflection, express caution, demand focus and direction, challenge flamboyance, facilitate direct communication, point out possible undertones

Transformations. Using this as a base, it has not been difficult to ascribe numbers to each of the skills classified. The Phase Two chart (Figure 19), especially the upper portion of it, is based on the Bellows-Post model. The bottom portion of the chart deals with action strategies. As one will usually want the adult natal year strength to be dominant, *supportive* strategies are suggested to activate those strengths. Where child natal month responses are evident and a supervisor or evaluator considers that it is a transition situation, *enhancing* strategies are recommended. *Controlling* strategies are recommended when an employee seems to be caught in habitual child responses, thus in their most stressful mode. All strategies are based on the mother–son transformation relationships and the ko (control) cycle.

As regards the strategies on the bottom of the chart, the purpose is not to manipulate people so much as to find a way that will actually help them to bring out their potential. As this is an energetic innovation, the suggestion here is to try the strategies to see how well they work rather than viewing and applying them in some dogmatic fashion. For one thing, people relate to their adult and child natal energetics according to circumstances, conditioning, etc. My experience is that once a person discovers what their actual energetic potentials are, a greater fluidity of expression emerges.

For Phase Two, all the birth-dates of the employees are needed. The birth-dates and Nine Star Ki birth-date configurations of the employees of our example are presented here:

Jane:	11 August 1961	3*m* (8*m*)one*m*
Jim:	5 July 1964	9*f*(1*m*)six*m*
Mike:	13 January 1962	3*m* (3*m*)five*m*/f
Dorothy:	11 April 1934	3*m* (3*m*)five*m*/f
Dave:	22 July 1963	1*m* (3*m*)seven*f*
John:	27 November 1961	3*m* (5*m*/f)seven
Tanya:	10 January 1955	1*m* (6*m*)one*m*
Denise:	20 April 1951	4*f*(6*m*)seven*f*

Using the chart, the strengths and weaknesses of each individual in the lab can be noted. The adult natal year number is written in capitals and the child natal month number is written in lower case letters. It should be borne in mind that adult traits are those from which the individual's greatest sense of strength and self-expression will emerge. The child traits are also skills and potentials, but they are subject to more past conditioning, as well as being a potential source for stress. Where the adult and child numbers are the same, as in our example with Mike and Dorothy, their individual tasks are to overcome their past conditioning in order to turn what is a potential source of stress into a strength.

As can be observed in the chart of lab employees, there is a dominance of planners (threes), both in adult and child expression. This group has a lot of ideas about almost every phase of the lab's activities. Endless possibilities may be discussed as to what could be done, with no particular goal in mind. Conversations may be loud, gestures bold, with an air of excitement, but this may have little to do with what is actually attained in the process. In terms of stress, irritation and frustration may be quite marked. Impatience and anger may dominate transactions with authority. As three-tree is the most independent of the numbers, this could easily be a case of 'too many chiefs, not enough Indians'.

The only other concentration in the chart is in the one-water area. Here there are two 'adults', Dave and Tanya, and one 'child', Jim. This is a group which is capable of seeing how things have gone, getting a sense of what is needed to change direction and providing encouragement and direction for all the planners in the group to investigate. As regards the group dynamic, although we shall go into this more in Phase Two, it is useful for this group to have a concentration in this area as it provides some sense of support for all the threes, as well as the supervisor.

If we look at the decision-making, interestingly enough, we find that the one who needs to focus the group, clarify and structure what actually goes on, turns out to be the supervisor, Denise. When it comes to getting things done, however, the group is lacking. Nine-fire people can catalyse things and bring them into some form, but it is in the areas of earth (two, five and eight) and metal/air (six and seven), that the consolidation, maturation and end products emerge. In the earth position, we have John and Jane who can get on in this area, but because it is their child natal month expression, it is a strain (not to mention the fact that their tree/space adult natal numbers have a controlling, hence limiting, effect on their earth expression). John and Jane may, in fact, find that much of their time and effort goes into worry and caretaking for the emotional needs of the group rather than the actual completion of tasks.

Tanya can put the final touches on things, balance efforts and be somewhat supportive to the supervisor, Denise. However, neither Tanya nor Denise comes out of a position of strength (that is, adult expression) in this situation. Tanya and Denise may find that much of their effort goes into trying to establish order, finding themselves on the defensive and putting an inordinate amount of time into dealing with the three-tree/space energy that dominates the group. Denise may find that she views situations in black and white terms, always being pushed to state the bottom line. And there is no one in the seven-metal/air position to act as an evaluator as the process of the group unfolds.

Phase Three

There are two ways to look at and evaluate data in Phase Three. First of all what is needed is a Five Transformation chart upon which the individual's natal adult and child numbers can be plotted. In dealing with a group, each individual's interactions with other members can be plotted on a one-to-one basis, as in our couple's example of John and Jennifer. This is certainly useful in assisting individuals in their interactions with the others in the group. However, a Five Transformation chart, where all individuals are plotted at once, best serves an evaluator or supervisor in looking at overall group dynamics. Although we shall look at the Five Transformation map more closely, the one-to-one model is still useful to have in so far as individuals do run into problems with each other that are more specific than could be explained by a group gestalt. (The one-to-one model would be used by taking one individual, let us say Jane, and making maps and couple-type narratives of her in relation to Jim, Mike, Dorothy, etc.)

Figure 20 shows a Five Transformation chart for the cardiovascular lab.

The basic theme of the lab staff is excitement and ideas. There is an endless stream of new ideas that people generate in this group – and a lot of talk about those ideas. The air is therefore usually charged. If it is charged in a negative way, rather than there being ideas and excitement, there can be agitation, anger and a chaotic feeling about daily operations.

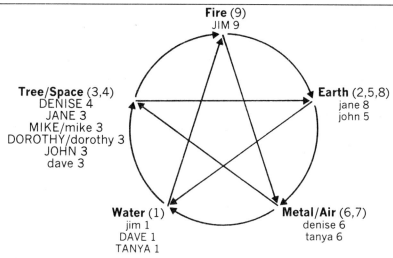

Figure 20. A Five Transformation chart for the Merrian Hill Center

When expressing their adult natal characteristics more, this group holds together. This does not mean that there are no problems, but they are more internal and personal than relational. Social interaction runs smoothly as water (Dave, Tanya and Jim) supports tree/space (Denise, Jim, Mike, Dave and Dorothy), which in turn supports fire (Jim). While this dominance of water, tree/space and fire creates a supportive network, it does not lead to a coordinated or consistent effort in the accomplishment of tasks. As three-trees are usually animatedly busy, there can be an appearance of accomplishment, while the effort is disproportionate to the actual results.

Internal and personal areas of tension arise where child natal numbers are activated or are in control positions relative to adult natal numbers. This is also true where child and adult numbers are the same.

Jane and John may be the task completers for the group, but this role is a strain on them in that it is a manifestation of their child natal energetics. They also put a lot of pressure on themselves as their adult natal tree/space aspect controls their child natal earth aspect. Dorothy and Mike, whose House of Five position gives them an earth quality, may also expend a lot of energy in task completion, but not without a lot of internal pressures as well.

These four are the workhorses of the group, but generally they do not feel good about it, either consciously or unconsciously. Their internal pressures and stress may be projected outwards in which case they can feel judged or watched over by the other three- and four-tree/space members of the group. This may create a feeling of resentment or a type of co-dependency where because the other three-tree-space numbers either identify with or go through the same internal dynamics, they can all unite in complaining about how stressful the situation is, how hard the work is and how insensitive the supervisor (Denise) is. It may be difficult for them to see that they are themselves the authors of their clash with authority, that they naturally have this struggle because of their tree/space and earth configurations. Moreover, it is a fact that unless they can run their own show, three-tree space individuals will inevitably run into difficulties with anyone or anything that inhibits their autonomy or independence.

Their situation is not helped by the fact that three-tree/space and four-tree/space people do not see eye to eye and there is some tension in their interaction. Here, the supervisor, Denise, tries to clarify and put order into what Jane, John, Dorothy and Mike generate. She may at times see what it is that they are trying to accomplish, but not why it has to be done the way it is being done. Denise likes to do one thing at a time and the timing of what is done is important for her. Likewise, her job makes time management a signpost to demonstrate effective cost and task supervision. To her, the way three-tree/space people operate seems time-consuming if not random – even chaotic.

Because her communication with three-tree/space people goes awry at times, she may easily slip into her six-metal/air child patterns. Her four-tree/space skills of initiating conflict may thus snap into open confrontation, where she makes black-and-white declarations of how she wants to run things. Sensing her weakness in such an approach as, again, this is not a dominant (i.e. adult natal) strength for her, her employees may not take her seriously and may just brush her off. Because her suggestions in this situation arise out of her stress and are usually mundane or consolidating, the three-trees will usually find them at best uninteresting and at worst an insult to their sense of brilliance and spaciousness.

What can temper and bring balance in this particular arena of conflict is Denise's relationship with Dave and Jim. Generally, Jim feels supportive both of the three-tree space team members and of four-tree space Denise. Jim finds Denise supportive, especially as he can be a catalysing force for the tree/space ideas generated and can keep operations moving forward. As regards the three-tree group, Jim may find that in times of crisis, he becomes their spokesman to Denise. As Jim feels supported by both the group and Denise, he may find himself in a quandary and not know where to stand. If Denise's six-metal child is activated in an attempt to control three-tree energy, Jim may become confrontational. His adult nine-fire energy may keep Denise's six-metal at bay, in which case she may become empowered to use more adult metal strategies. It all depends on how safe Jim feels in his relationship with Denise. There is a tendency, however, for Jim to retreat into his one-water position of cautiousness and reserve. Denise's six-metal behaviour may even activate Jim's one-water child tendencies.

As regards Dave, Denise's six-metal behaviour in times of stress may activate Dave's one-water adult. As water supports tree/space and Dave's child is a three-tree/space, he can identify with the group tensions, but can act as a support for both the group and Denise by reflecting back to them what he sees and possibly acting as a bridge between the group and Denise. This, of course, depends on how much Dave identifies with his adult or child characteristics. If he is living out of his child (three-tree/space) expression, which is his tendency as his one-water adult precipitates a three-tree/space expression, he may just identify with the three-tree/space crowd, in which case, because his three-tree/space is his child expression, he may be the most vocal in dissent.

Another area of energetic interaction revolves around Dave, Tanya and Jim. As I have said, Jim has a tendency to become less expressive in the group as his one-water child cautiousness can undermine his nine-fire adult potentials. This tendency is reinforced by both Dave and Tanya. Jim may feel that Dave has some influence on him, but there is a controlling aspect to this. At the same time, Dave's three-tree/space child traits may lead him to look to Jim as a source of inspiration, especially to help him with his frustration at times. The resulting dynamic may make Jim feel that Dave idealizes or has great expectations of him.

Tanya likewise reinforces Jim's water tendencies, but equally feels under pressure from Jim as her six-metal child is controlled by Jim's nine-fire adult. As Tanya identifies with and can feel under pressure from Jim, his actions from his nine-fire adult potential, may lead her to doubt herself. This may lead her to put more pressure on him, in which case their relationship may be an insidious triangle of energetics that leaves both feeling stultified.

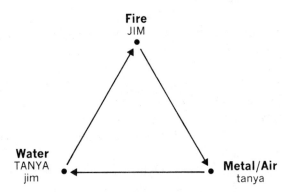

Figure 21. A Five Transformation chart for Tanya and Jim.

This particular triangle has the potential for being the most volatile in the group process. However, this all depends on how much Jim acts out of his nine-fire adult potential. If he experiences his water transformation as more dominant, then Tayna's six-metal child and one-water adult are nurturing and reinforcing an identification with his child potentials, in which case Jim's effectiveness in the group will be greatly reduced.

In Tanya, the supervisor Denise may find her greatest ally. Tanya can either identify with or be supportive of Denise in child and adult aspects respectively. When under stress, both Tanya and Denise have similar responses and thus may reinforce each other in their child natal expression. However, Tanya can slip out of this pattern more easily, coming into her one-water adult aspect. As water is the mother of tree/space, Tanya's adult expression, her ability to reflect, respond with consideration and communicate well with all tree/space individuals, may provide Denise with the kind of clarity and support she needs to come back into her adult four-tree/space expression.

A final comment needs to be made regarding the tree/space energetics within this group. The natural air of excitement and ideas holds a lot of positive possibilities for the group. However, since three people have their child aspects in this position (Mike, Dorothy and Dave), there is a strong likelihood that the group will lapse into frustration and dissent. This will, in turn, undermine group spontaneity, sabotage Jane and John's efforts, starve Jane of support and put Denise on the defensive, where she issues ultimatums that only Tanya is willing to accept.

Phase Four

The strategies within Phase Four can vary according to the group being addressed and the circumstances in which it operates. Recommendations can be of a relational nature, such as how to address specific personal dynamics or general group interaction patterns, or circumstantial, in which case suggestions made may include activities and environmental changes.

In the case of the cardiovascular lab, without making staff changes it is imperative that supervisory efforts be made to tap into the creative energy of three-tree/space that dominates the group. It is with this foremost in mind that the following recommendations are made.

1. Dave and Tanya should be encouraged to share their perspective on the overall running and atmosphere of the lab. Their reflections and comments could be used as a basis for inspiring Jim, Mike, Dorothy, John and Denise. Communications between these one-water adults and the three- and four-tree/space group may need to be encouraged, especially as it is in the nature of one-water people to be cautious in what they present to others and how they do it. Once Dave and Tanya have presented to the others, feedback from Jane, Mike, Dorothy and John should be encouraged to ensure that what Dave and Tanya have shared is clearly understood.

2. Give the three-tree/space adults a diversity of tasks. Use them for brainstorming new ways of operating. Get them to learn all the different jobs in the lab so that they can not only fill in for one another, but possibly even change positions at will from time to time.

3. Encourage Jim to overcome his caution and 'run with the ball'; to catalyse whatever it is that Jane, Mike, Dorothy and John come up with. Ideas from Mike, Dorothy and Dave may at times be impulsive, because of their attempts to overcome self-doubt (especially Mike and Dorothy), but Jim should hear them out. His comments and actions on their suggestions may improve their overall response in the group.

4. In times of stress, Mike, Dorothy and Dave may be the focal group for frustration and anger within the lab. To balance this tendency, meetings should be arranged where the adult three-tree/space qualities of Jane and John are utilized, together with the structuring and conflict management skills of Denise. Tanya can provide support for a more mature approach from Dave and support others in allowing the adult, rather than the child, quality of the three-tree/space transformation to emerge. She can also be a helpful ally for Denise.

5. Given the fact that no one in the lab is in an adult earth or metal/air position energetically to complete tasks, Jim should be encouraged to provide moral support to John, Jane and Tanya in their efforts. What may thwart this is that Jane can lapse into hopelessness and John into indecisiveness and worry given their three-tree/space controlling adult energetics. However, because they also naturally empower Jim, they may be able to over-ride their personal tendencies as they interact with him. Jim's relationship to Tanya may not directly support task completion. However, it may help her to overcome her tendency to take on too much responsibility and any sense of guilt in her functioning in the lab.

6. This staff team has a lot of physical energy. People should be encouraged to take exercise at lunch time, or at least once a day. Organize group walks or even stress management sessions where stretching, breathing and relaxation exercises are taught. Rechannelling such physical energy will improve morale and relations. Even the encouragement of a good hug between workers during the day may go a long way in breaking up any tension. (This is based on the fact that the primary ways in which three-tree/space people feel nurtured is through touch and contact.)

7. With a dominance of three-tree/space energy in the group, lighting, colour and a sense of spaciousness in the working environment are important. Lighting should be as natural as

possible; replace fluorescent bulbs with full-spectrum and incandescent ones. There should be green and blue colours throughout the physical space – plants would be a good idea. Water and tree/space people are sensitive to electromagnetic influences. Computer display terminals should have protective screening and be turned off when not in use. The use of asynchronous natural sound and music can also help to mellow the naturally intense atmosphere that such a group generates.

8. A suggestion box and other means of facilitating the expression of the constant flood of ideas coming from the team is essential. Innovation need not imply revolution. However, if one does not acknowledge their innovative ways, there will be revolutions.

9. When interviewing for new staff in the future, look for more earth and metal/air adults. Being service-oriented, they will enhance the success and bring balance to the lab and staff.

◆ One Step Further: Birth Charts for Organizations, Groups and Events

As I said in the Introduction, all things must go through a process conception, gestation, maturation and manifestation. This applies to both the animal and the vegetable kingdoms.

In the realm of human beings, it also applies to our endeavours. For example, two people meet, they like each other, they court and they get married – the marriage being a manifest statement of their love for each other. The same applies to a business or organization. A person or a group gets an idea, they work out the details, and, at some point, that idea becomes an entity – a product or enterprise of some sort.

In the Orient, the time at which one establishes an enterprise or embarks upon a venture is not left to chance. Astrologers are consulted for auspicious dates and times. Geomancers are consulted regarding the appropriate place, construction, etc. Recently, while living in Kentucky, I observed how a major Japanese motor car company which was trying to establish a plant in that state, used numerology and astrology to come up with the right place and the right offer at the right time. One can also ponder the actions of Ronald Reagan, who seemed to get apparently unpopular ideas approved, and to act in ways that probably would have caused more of a stir had he not chosen the right timing. People scorned the Reagans' use of astrology. Considering their success and popularity, however, it may behove others to look more closely at this approach and consider whether it is not more than mere superstition. In early 1991, the United States decided to go to war with Iraq. The deadline for the initiation of military action was set for 15 January of that year. Was it just coincidence that this day also corresponded to a new moon and a solar eclipse, and was a day that was very significant in Tibetan astrology?

Trying to arrange events in accordance with Nine Star Ki merely requires knowing how to calculate the numbers for given dates and what energetics you want to have present when the event occurs. The more you study the profiles, narratives and various aspects of the number combinations, the more you will have a clearer sense of what the dynamics will be at the time of the venture.

Besides this predictive quality, when analysing the dynamics of an event, group or enterprise that already exists, you can treat the origination date, be it an event, the date of incorporation of a company, or the signing of a contract, as the birth-date and calculate the dynamics present at the time just as you would do for an individual.

What is the value of such calculations for groups or businesses?

Just as individuals go through peak times, challenging times and low times, the same is true for any venture. In a business, you can see when operations have gone smoothly; when they have not; whether there are noticeable cycles in financial growth, times of expansion and times of recession or slow down; and whether there are times when personnel work better together than others.

Treating the origination date of a group or business as a birth-date, you can also look at the dynamics of the enterprise as an entity in relation to the people working for it. Given the dynamics of an enterprise, how have individuals within that enterprise functioned? Are they well placed? How can you create a more cohesive support system for your enterprise?

The implications of using Nine Star Ki in such a manner are far-reaching. Not only can a business or organization be steered in accordance with the energetics of the time, but changes needed within (such as staff appointments, re-configurations, hirings or redundancies) can be tailored to give the optimal internal dynamics for the desired external results, whether they be increased production, profit or anything else.

◆ Some General Remarks

After making such detailed observations of individual and group behaviours and listing specific recommendations as found in Phase Four the steering of a group in such a way may often seem awkward or contrived. In order to manifest our adult natal potentials, there has to be a sense of personal empowerment, a certain level of basic confidence and trust in who we are. When this is not present, it is an indication that our child natal potentials persist and may even dominate our lives on various levels. To create an atmosphere in a group process where the adult natal potentials are expressed more than the child potentials and the resultant personal stress patterns is a challenge, but it is necessary for healthy personal and interpersonal growth and interaction. Thus it is a goal worth pursuing.

One of the first issues that needs to be addressed in working towards this goal is to confront the denial that the group is operating out of the child natal patterns. In fact, denial promotes elevated stress and disease – more so even than the child natal energetics themselves. Confrontation of this denial can take the form of any number of strategies, the intention of which is to make it less and less of a viable option in our behaviour and ways of thinking. Once the breakthrough is achieved and we get in touch with and can accept the way that we are living our lives, the space created in our expression gives room for the adult natal characteristics to emerge.

My personal observation in seeing this happen is that individuals in a group are hesitant at first, begin gradually to see and experience the truth of Nine Star Ki, and then express in a more whole-hearted way traits and ways of being that feel new, yet natural at the same time. It is almost as if a large burden had been lifted from their shoulders. Then people learn to naturally assert themselves, no longer apologizing for who they are.

Not apologizing for who they are does not mean that they become pig-headed or obnoxious in their interactions. In fact, I have observed that as people accept themselves more, they relax, become less defensive and have more compassion and time for those around them. So much of the pain in relating is our own self-uncertainty and projected neuroses. As these become less solid, the barriers between individuals become less and less significant. Openness, humour and inquisitiveness emerge as natural ways of interacting.

This does not mean that the adult natal way of being doesn't possess challenges. It is just that being personally empowered, being in and relating to the world we live in is less of an effort. There may still be exertion. There remains the fact that the combinations of some transformation energetics are smoother than others, both within our own being and when relating to others. But whereas effort implies history and working against or in spite of something – usually limitations we impose on ourselves or think others are imposing on us (more often than not, a projection) – exertion in its purest sense is dynamic, present-moment, intentional movement. The past is no longer something that we have to work our way out of. Rather it becomes a foundation upon which new and creative directions in our lives can be built.

A Final Word

In Part 1, I explained how our migration through the years and all their transformations gave us the opportunity to experience and appreciate life in all its possible elemental permutations. We are given a chance to become whole, mature individuals just by remaining open to what life offers us. The special gift of relating to others is that this whole process is speeded up. Rather than waiting for the changing of the days, months and years, each individual that walks into our lives provides us with an on-the-spot opportunity to expand and share in a dance, a weaving and blending of natal energetics and potentials that can enrich our lives, if we only remain open and allow ourselves to view the world in wholeness, rather than in separation.

Opening our hearts and minds the fiction of separation dissolves of its own accord. In the end, the way we relate to ourselves is the way we relate to our world and to others. If we do not see ourselves as separate from the world or other people, then we are not. If that is so, then every moment and every interaction becomes a spontaneous expression of life, of transformational forces in a beautiful, harmonious dance. As we embrace others in this spirit, we embrace the world and ourselves.

Towards that end, may this book be of benefit.

Anecdote:
A Personal Account
by Marcia Sutton, PhD

'How was your dream trip to Europe, Marcia?' I was asked many times when I returned from two months of field research in Italy, France and the British Isles in the summer of 1990. My friends expected a positive answer, rave reviews. After all, how could it be a hardship to visit Europe's ancient sacred places to gather data for a forthcoming book.

But it *was* hard, up to a point.

Before leaving home, I had received a Nine Star Ki astrology reading from my friend Bob Sachs. The reading showed an amazing pattern when it was overlaid on my European itinerary. Without exception, every time I planned to turn north, east, south or west, I would be facing a difficult or troublesome aspect. I would not be in danger, but wonderful experiences (the norm of my life) wouldn't be plentiful either. Never mind. I had planned this trip for a year and I would proceed, even though the preparations had become tedious rather than fun. It *had* to be the right time to go, because I could, I wanted to, I would do it.

It was uncanny how the timing and directions of my itinerary pointed me at the most taxing aspects of myself every time. Bob said I would be facing my adult self. I could meet the challenges as a wanting, needing child and feel affronted, or I could meet them as a capable, mature person and grow with each opportunity.

Before leaving home, as I absorbed this astrological reading, of course I assumed that I would take the mature path. Once I was on the road, however, I did not always feel I had the strength to be so objective.

So what happened? I was to leave on Monday, after turning in grades the previous Friday for the courses I taught at the university. That week, my eighty-year-old father was suddenly hospitalized and needed a pacemaker. Was this a sign that I should stay in the States? I flew to Pennsylvania to be with him and then went on to London. But in London, there was no hotel reservation for me because the travel agent had not confirmed it in writing. That hotel was full but they found me a room nearby. On a hunch I phoned ahead to Paris to my next hotel: no reservation because of no written confirmation, but they would make room for me for a night or two. Fine.

A world-famous museum in London that I had waited a decade to see was disappointing; the exhibits I was most interested in were not on display. The old church of the Knights Templar was closed. But many things went right. The weather was decent. The Underground was an efficient transport system. Two 'walking tours' of old London revealed fascinating, mysterious parts of the city. Next stop, Paris.

The same pattern occurred. Fortunate events (such as getting the last ticket to a flamenco dance appearance) were balanced by unfortunate events (such as the most important window in Chartres Cathedral having been removed for cleaning, my hotel being torn apart for remodelling and the parrots in the breakfast room gone, being shoved out of line by German tourists).

By this time I realized that my biggest mistake was to think I could wrench myself away from my network of loving family and friends without emotional loss. I had never been so lonely! I had never needed comfort and support so badly. I had expected to meet lots of 'interesting people' but everyone seemed to be connected already except me. Every single person I had planned to see, whether friend or professional contact, couldn't make it: sick/phone disconnected/out of town – the reasons varied but the result was the same. When I found out that the Dalai Lama would be in northern Italy the same week that I was there, I tried every way to rearrange my schedule so I could see him. But there were no hotel rooms, or when he would be close enough for me to travel by train or bus for a day trip, he was not having any public audiences that day.

I was catching on to the meaning of the astrological reading. A series of small challenges was coming at me like tennis balls: here, hit this one. Here, field that one. The trip continued like that for weeks.

My husband joined me for a tour of France. We were disappointed at the Disney-World atmosphere pervading the more famous sacred sites we visited. This wouldn't do at all for the book I had in mind.

This buffeting of good and ill fortune went on until I re-routed myself. Instead of going to Spain as planned, my husband and I reversed direction and went to England. From that moment on, our fortunes improved. We spent time at powerful sacred sites, so remote and uncommercialized that one had to hunt diligently in the fog to locate them. We had a seaside picnic on a cliff at Land's End, stayed in a big Victorian room, drove down country lanes so narrow that the mirrors on both sides of the car were brushed by the growing crops. We were touched by the beauty and the mystery of the sites we were privileged to visit and the people who were making similar pilgrimages.

So when my friends back home asked how my trip had been, I answered, 'Difficult, memorable, challenging, well worth it. I learned as much about myself as I did about the sacred places of Europe.'

APPENDICES

1 ◆ *Aspects of the Five Transformations*

Element	Tree/Space	Fire	Earth	Metal/Air	Water
Season	Spring	Early Summer	Late Summer Solstices & Equinoxes	Autumn	Winter
Colour	Green	Red	Yellow	White	Black
Direction	East	South	Centre	West	North
Associated Nine Star Ki Numbers	3, 4	9	2, 5, 8	6, 7	1
Associated Yin organs	Gall Bladder	Small Intestine, Triple Warmer	Stomach	Large Intestine	Bladder
Associated Yang organs	Liver	Heart, Heart Governor	Spleen/Pancreas	Lungs	Kidneys
Time of day activated	Gall Bladder (11pm–1am) Liver (1am–3am)	Small Intestine (1–3pm) Triple Warmer (9–11pm) Heart (11am–1pm) Heart Governor (7–9pm)	Stomach (7–9am) Spleen/Pancreas (9–11am)	Lower Intestine (5–7am) Lungs (3–5am)	Bladder (3–5pm) Kidneys (5–7pm)
Associated body formation	Connective Tissue, Muscles	Blood Vessels	Flesh	Skin, Body Hair	Bones, Head Hair
Associated sense organ	Eye (Sight)	Tongue (Speech)	Mouth (Taste)	Nose (Smell)	Ears (Hearing)
Associated secretion	Tears	Sweat	Saliva	Mucus	Urine
Taste	Sour	Bitter	Sweet	Pungent	Salty
Emotion (& extremes)	Irritability (Anger)	Joy (Hysteria)	Empathy (Obsessiveness)	Reflection (Sentimentality)	Caution (Fear)
Voice expression	Shout	Laugh	Sing	Weep	Groan
Faculty	Spiritual	Inspirational	Intellectual	Vital	Will
Illness first detected in	Throat & Neck	Chest & Ribs	Spine	Shoulders & Back	Loins & Thighs
Time of acute problems	Spring	Early Summer	Any Time	Autumn	Winter
Time of chronic problems	Autumn	Winter	Any Time	Spring	Summer
Celestial influence	Jupiter	Mars	Earth	Venus	Mercury

Figure 22. Aspects of the Five Transformations

2 ◆ *Theory Supporting Nine Star Ki*

◆ Heaven, Earth and Man: The Principle of Macrocosm and Microcosm

One of the basic principles implicit in Oriental thought is that we are a microcosm of a greater macrocosm: that we are integrally connected with the world that we perceive, that our outer world is a reflection of our inner world, and vice versa. The separation between the two is illusory. Distinctions between the seeming two are merely linguistically useful and mundanely convenient. If taken too literally or seriously the resulting dualism leads to all sorts of confusion, misunderstandings and a host of personal and planetary problems. Ultimately it is being ignorant of our inter-connectedness with our world that is the source of all our human mischief.

History tells of the many men and women throughout time and around the world who from a yearning for truth devised systems to explore both our inner and outer reality. Amongst those searchers were the philosophers and sages of the East who came to see that the laws that governed the energetic properties in nature applied not only to plants and animals, but to all life, including humans. For example, the I Ching arose out of an intuitive understanding of the relationship between what the literature describes as heaven, earth and man. Yearly and seasonal cycles, human psychology and physiology, social and political law and reform and the art of geomancy *feng shui*, to name a few aspects of life, all arise from a common knowledge base. Thus in describing politics it is not unusual to find metaphors from nature or human physiology. And it is not unusual for corollaries to be drawn from one aspect of nature to another. That different aspects of reality share similar properties, energetics and ways of functioning is one way the sages were able to prove the macro-cosmic/microcosmic premiss.

◆ The Energetics of Nature, Acupuncture Theory, and the Five Transformations

One of the most profound of ancient sciences was the under-standing of energetics and principles of change as found in the acupuncture system. This system was not only for understanding human functioning, ailments and cures, but it also had a cosmic vision.

Masters of this system observed that there is a central magnetic-ally charged core to the human form: an electromagnetic field running from the crown of the head to a point just behind the scrotum in a man or back of the vagina in a woman. There is a positive and a negative pole to this core. Around this core are two central electrical lines (or meridians – the acupuncture term) constantly circulating the energy from this charged central core. Off these two primary meridians arise the twelve other major meridians that are either more positively or more negatively charged. These twelve form the electromagnetic basis for the growth, sustenance, and demise of all major body organs, systems and their related functions. These meridians are not a random phenomenon, but a power grid which runs throughout the body, on the body's surface and out to a distance of one hand span from the body surface. There are circuit breakers – areas of low electri-cal impulse – along all of these meridians. These are the acupunc-ture points.

The central core of the body runs at about a 23° tilt from the polar end at our heads to the polar end between our legs. Interest-ingly enough, this is the same tilt as the Earth has on its axis as it moves through space. We also know that there are electromagne-tic lines which weave around the Earth's North and South Poles. The Van Allen belts are akin to the body's aura. Ley lines – known to earth mystics, geomancers, and diviners – are like the Earth's acupuncture meridians with sacred or power spots like the body's acupuncture points. (It is even interesting to see how over such points, civilizations have erected pyramids, obelisks and various monolithic structures as if they were giant acupuncture needles pulling in cosmic energies in the same way that needles applied to the body's acupuncture points are used to stabilize the electromagnetic force in a meridian by changing or draining it.)

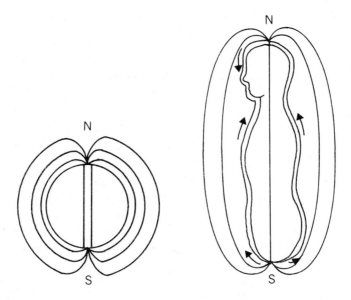

Figure 23. The electromagnetic fields of earth and man

    As the human electromagnetic patterns are similar to planetary electromagnetic patterns, it stands to reason that if planetary electromagnetic patterns are altered, a similar shift would be observed on the microcosmic (human) level. And although Chinese and other Oriental sages were not familiar with the language of modern physics, their keen sense of observation led them to detect subtle changes in the electromagnetic forces around them; changes that have a cyclical nature, affecting plants, animals, human characteristics, consciousness and interaction, and the world in general.

    The electromagnetic forces in nature and in the human form undergo five seemingly distinct but interdependent transformation phases. These are the gestation, maturation, consolidation, completion and resting phases. The Chinese acupuncture theory gives these transformations more elemental names: wood or space, fire, earth, metal or air, and water respectively. All life forms, be they plant or animal (including human), go through and are embodiments of all these elemental transformations. And while a plant or animal may be more obviously going through one particular transformation phase, all the other phases are present on a more subtle level. From the most observable expressions of living organisms right down to the cellular level, these transformations are going on continuously.

At the same time, while all these transformations can be observed in all things, each has its own seat – a place or system in which the particular way in which a transformative phase expresses itself is more dominant. Thus, in the case of humans there are organs, systems and ways of being in the world that are – in the language of acupuncture – more wood/space-like, fire-like, earth-like, etc. (When we speak of organs, systems and ways of being, we include levels of consciousness, as Oriental thought does not draw a distinction between physiological and psychological, or body and mind, manifestations and functions. All physiological and psychological phenomena, including body gestures, speech and inflections, thought dominance – to name but a few – are linked and interdependent in a way that is observable and classifiable in accordance with the Chinese Law of Five Transformations.)

Oriental sages observed that although these Five Transformations are taking place continuously, there are variations in the dominance of one transformation over the others according to time: the time of day and the months and seasons as well as the years. Each hour of the day is dominated by either wood/space, fire, earth, metal/air or water transformative-type energy. Spring is associated with wood or space; early and mid-summer with fire; solstices, equinoxes and late summer with earth; autumn with metal or air; and winter with water.

To live in accordance with the cycles of the days, the months and the seasons helps to create balance and health on a day-to-day basis. However, sages could also see that the larger cycles, and more particularly a cycle of nine years, has a more profound and lasting influence on our condition and basic psycho-physical constitution.

◆ Why Nine Star and what is Ki?

Although our planet's polar axis is tilted at 23° with the star Polaris in Ursa Minor above its northern pole, this is not a constant. Modern astronomers know that approximately every 26,000 years the Earth 'flops' to a position where the star Vega in the constellation Lyra becomes the pole star. This shift is fairly dramatic. However, there is a less dramatic wobbling that our planet makes on its axis, a wobbling that invariably alters the north-south polarity.

Sages of the past were able to observe nine distinguishable electromagnetic phases in this wobbling. Astrology and astronomy were both sciences in those days, so it was determined that as there are nine stars in the northern sky closely centred around the northern end of the Earth's polar axis – Polaris, Vega and the seven stars that make up Ursa Major (the Big Bear) – they are responsible for the slight electromagnetic shift that occurs. Thus, as Nine Star Ki theory has it, each star is integrally a part of and responsible for each of the distinguishable electromagnetic phases.

When our planet is under the influence of one of the particular electromagnetic phases, one of the transformation phases or transformations mentioned earlier becomes accentuated. Thus there are fire years, earth years, water years, and so on with all elemental or transformation phases represented within a nine-year cycle. The cycle begins with a fire year, followed by an earth year, followed by two metal/air years, followed by an earth year, then two wood/space years, another earth year, and finally a water year which leads us back into another fire year to begin a new cycle. As particular transformations are accentuated from year to year, so it is also that each of the transformation's more positive and negative charges is accentuated. This leads us into a brief discussion of yin, yang and ki.

'Ki' must first be mentioned. This is the Japanese term for *chi* in Chinese, and *prana* in Sanskrit. Roughly translated into English it is 'life force'. It is a force that pervades all of life. It is associated with consciousness and the will. Its source is the subject of philosophical and theological speculation. It is the mastery of 'ki' which is at the central core of martial arts. The various yogic systems of Buddhism, Hinduism, Taoism and other traditions utilize the awareness of this subtle force and our ability to work with it in order to achieve the end states or realization as perceived by such systems.

On a fairly crude level, the presence of ki is detected by the presence of an electromagnetic force, which again is detected on subtle or crude levels: the aura, the psychic channels and vortices (chakras) of the body, the acupuncture meridian system, the autonomic system and finally the central nervous system. Such electromagnetic force is only noticeable when there is a slightly more positive or negative charge present. And for movement and life to be present, there must be a continuous fluctuation in the dominance of positive and negative charges. The acupuncture system goes on to point out that with a more positive charge, life forms or functions seem to go into a relatively more contractive state as opposed to a more expanded, relaxed state when the negative charge is dominant. Using the macrobiotic theories of George Ohsawa we classify the positive/contractive state as being yang and the negative/expansive state as being yin. This differs from classical Chinese acupuncture theory, which would reverse the terminology. This does not alter the functional or usable aspects of this theory, so the macrobiotic interpretation is what I have used in this volume.

◆ Yin and Yang

Nothing is solely yin. Nothing is solely yang. The flow of ki means that the apparent opposite is present when there is a positive or a negative electromagnetic dominance.

Figure 24. The yin/yang symbol

In Figure 24, we are looking at a static representation of yin and yang force. If we were to look at each one of the transformation phases, we would see a dominance of either the lighter area (yang) or the darker area (yin). Even then, such a representation would need a third dimension to demonstrate the subtlety of this system.

To summarize briefly, life force or ki pervades all life and is detected or experienced in a relatively more yin or yang state. The fluctuation between yin and yang is continuous, with certain states of balance represented as one of the Five Transformations. As our planet wobbles through space, the ki flow of our world is altered. Thus different transformation phases with a relatively more yin or yang expression of the ki flow become accentuated.

Being interested in systems and ways of codifying data within systems, sages who worked with the Five Transformations and the laws of yin and yang began at some point in time – perhaps in accordance with the history presented – to ascribe numerical values to each of the transformations. Numerical values and the construction of lined trigrams and hexagrams representing numerical value – hence transformations – is the basis of the I Ching, probably the most complete presentation of Chinese thought and source from which a *fully systematized* Nine-House or Nine Star Ki astrological system emerged. Thus, when looking at a Nine Star Ki astrological chart, rather than seeing elements or signs as in other astrological systems, one sees a system of numbers that have been systematically calculated for a given individual.

Figure 25 shows all nine years of a cycle with transformation phase, yin/yang dominance, numerical value and trigram structure.

The Nine Star Ki system most widely used has the numbers and their respective transformation phases descending in order through time, nine to one. Nine (fire) is considered the most yin or expanded number with each successive number being more contracted, even though the numbers become more intense as they approach 'one', each number reveals a more yielding or open (yin), or active and insular (yang) side to its nature. Figure 26 is a graph of the cycle of nine years based on the contracting movement with yin and yang variations.

Transformation Phase (Element)	Ying/Yang	Number	Trigram	
Fire	Yin	9	☲	(Li)
Earth	Yang	8	☶	(Ken)
Air/Metal	Yin	7	☱	(Tui)
Air/Metal	Yang	6	☰	Ch'ien)
Earth	Yin/Yang	5	none	
Tree/Space	Yin	4	☴	(Sun)
Tree/Space	Yang	3	☳	(Chen)
Earth	Yin	2	☷	(K'un)
Water	Yang	1	☵	(K'an)

Figure 25. The relationship between year number and transformation phase

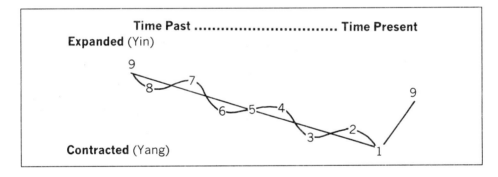

Figure 26. Nine years along a time continuum

Excluding the peculiarities of each of the transformation phases for a moment, the general trend of intensification of the years over a nine-year cycle can be observed. For example there are years when we feel that events and our lives are moving rather slowly, other years when they move more quickly. It could be argued that this is a subjective experience, that it just has to do with our personal experience. However, there is another level of subjectivity: our basic human experience which transcends our individual subjective peculiarities. It is this level of subjectivity that we are addressing.

On a more observable level, sages noted that certain vegetation and animal life was more dominant or active, relatively speaking, in a particular year. They would see how in one year apples or carrots might be more prolific while in other years they would do poorly while squashes and melons did well. This was observed to have more to do with yearly cycles than with the results of human effort.

As with the plant or animal kingdoms – and here more specifically human beings – it was noted that certain physiological and psychological characteristics are dominant in given years with changes of the months and years producing people of different qualities. For example, people born in certain years seem to be more physically agile than those born in other years. Some years, it was noted, produced people who are more philosophical; other years, natural born leaders. And in the life-span of any person, just like a carrot, there are easy months and years and difficult months and years, determined by the interaction of original birth characteristics with changes in transformation dominance in the cycle of months and years.

This is difficult for modern individualistic humans to accept only because of a basic lack of understanding of the world, an attachment to preconceived ideas and a determination to hold on to what seems familiar and deny anything or anyone that indicates the contrary. The resulting insensitivity to the inter-connectedness we have with the world around us puts us under the influence of arrogance – the function of our ignorance, attachment and aggression – where any serendipitous event or connections we feel towards others are regarded as the products of our individual efforts.

◆ The Special Quality of Nine Star Ki as an Astrological System

It is interesting to note that just as there are twelve houses or zodiac signs in conventional astrology, there are twelve major acupuncture meridians that run along the human body. Being electromagnetic in nature, as we saw earlier, the stars and planets within the conventional zodiacal system have their influence, and that influence can be far-reaching.

At the same time, acupuncture theory postulates that the general constitutional strengths of the twelve meridians of the body are determined by the yin/yang balance and ki flow of two other – and more central – meridians: the brain governor and the conception vessel. These two meridians run vertically along the central vertical plane of the body, the central core of which is the north/south polar axis of the body.

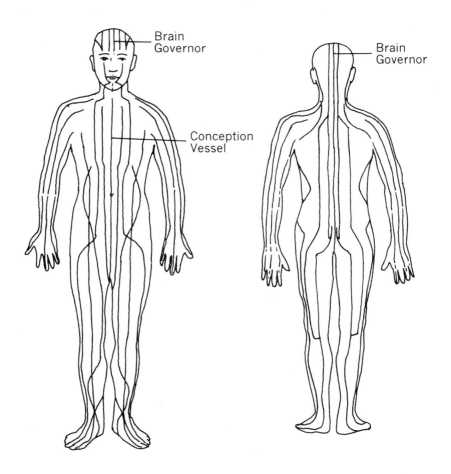

Brain Governor

Brain Governor

Conception Vessel

Figure 27. The two central meridians

Conventional astrology has always demonstrated the inter-connection between mind, body and spirit, pointing out how certain signs impact on certain organs, systems of the body or states of mind. This is true for Nine Star Ki as well. However, whereas one may find that one shares similar experiences and life situations with those of a similar astrological sign, the traits that one shares with others whose Nine Star Ki numbers are the same seem to run much deeper. The issue is no longer what one experiences, but how one experiences in the first place. 'What' implies product; 'how' implies process.

By analogy, whereas conventional astrology can present you a tapestry of your life, the images and quality of which you can learn to accept and move along with based on what is presented, Nine Star Ki is like looking directly at the quality of the threads within the images. If one knows the colours, textures and qualities of the threads, one has greater latitude in tightening or loosening the weave, even changing the image in so far as conditions allow. What both I and Nine Star Ki expert Rex Lassalle have observed is that sidereal-based astrologies, such as the Indian vedic system, come closest in being able to identify as central to a person's being, the core traits that are readily identified by the Nine Star Ki.

Like other astrological systems that speak of the migration of houses and coming under the dominance of various planets in various increments of time, this is also true of Nine Star Ki. What the ki takes into consideration is that given one's particular transformation phase dominances and the specific time frame with its dominant characteristics, obvious and fairly predictable ways of feeling and experiencing the world will occur, based on how various transformations interact as postulated in acupuncture theory. This adds texture to our basic ways of being and will be the backdrop upon which the events of our lives will be laid out. In *An Anthology of I Ching*, Sherrill and Chu summarize this point most appropriately and provide an excellent overview of the value and purpose of Nine Star Ki.

In Nine House astrology a man or woman is not simply born in a particular 'house', but during his or her lifetime migrates through the yearly, monthly, daily and hourly sequences many times. The belief behind this is that man can and should become as perfectly balanced as possible through facing and overcoming all the varied experience presented to him as a result of the influences of the various 'houses'. People follow different patterns because of the influences permanently imprinted upon them at their particular times of birth. The rules that carry them through these cycles remain constant, and it depends upon their state of wisdom as to how well they apply them. The different situations different people face are determined by their state of evolution at the time they re-enter this world. The strength and intensity of troubles or good fortune depend on the strength and (cosmic) maturity of the individual. These considerations lend Nine House astrology a philosophical aspect as well.[6]

3 ◆ The Twenty-Four Seasons

With this twenty-four season concept, the year is divided into thirteen months with shorter time increments around the winter solstice. Rather than starting the monthly calendar close to the start of the Chinese New Year, it begins right after the winter solstice. Thus the ascribing of natal month numbers at that time of year differs from Figure 5 on page 17. You are advised to see whether the chart in Figure 5 or the following chart based on one shown in Sherrill and Chu: *An Anthology of I Ching*, is more appropriate for you.

Approximate dates	In the year			24 Seasons
	1,4,7	2,5,8	3,6,9	
22 Dec–5 Jan	1	4	7	(1) winter solstice
6 Jan–3 Feb	9	3	6	(2) little cold (3) severe cold
4 Feb–5 Mar	8	2	5	(4) spring begins (5) rain water
6 Mar–4 Apr	7	1	4	(6) excited insects (7) vernal equinox
5 Apr–5 May	6	9	3	(8) clear and bright (9) grain rains
6 May–5 Jun	5	8	2	(10) summer begins (11) grain fills
6 Jun–7 Jul	4	7	1	(12) grain in ears (13) summer solstice
8 Jul–7 Aug	3	6	9	(14) slight heat (15) great heat
8 Aug–7 Sep	2	5	8	(16) autumn begins (17) limit of heat
8 Sep–8 Oct	1	4	7	(18) white dew (19) autumnal equinox
9 Oct–7 Nov	9	3	6	(20) cold dew (21) hoar frost descends
8 Nov–7 Dec	8	2	5	(22) winter begins (23) little snow
8 Dec–21 Dec	7	1	4	(24) heavy snow

Figure 28.
Descending natal month numbers according to the twenty-four season concept.

4 ◆ Descending and Ascending Numbers Through Time: a Consideration for Women

Although the descending order of numbers from nine to one through the years is used for both men and women in the Japanese system, this is not so in the Chinese system. The direction of numbers from nine to one is considered to be an overall contracting (yang) direction, even though there are both expanding (yin) and contracting (yang) variations in the numbers movement. The Chinese considered this yang direction to be more masculine and hence ascribed it to men (as yang is associated with masculine/male energy). For them, therefore, there also had to be a more yin or expanding cycle within the years – and numbers – over time that would be best suited to feminine energy. Thus the numbers for women are considered to go in the opposite direction, that is one to nine through the years, with the number three being the only year common to men and women. This also means that in any given year there is, in this Chinese system, a different transformation phase that is dominant for men and women.

It has been my experience and the experience of Nine Star Ki specialist Rex Lassalle that the Japanese system of descending numbers through the years works best for both men and women as regards personal characteristics and stress patterns on both physiological and psychological levels. However, this may only be because of what appears to be the dominance of and emphasis on the masculine persona in this time period. This being the case, it may even be that women, on physiological and psychological levels, are sacrificing something innately feminine in their being, and are identifying – either consciously or unconsciously – with this persona. Thus they could manifest the same patterns or tendencies as their male counterparts of any particular year.

Taking this hypothesis out of a gender context, Nine Star Ki master Michio Kushi contends that the reason why the descending (yang) order works best for both men and women in this time is that the yang order represents a more materialistic way of being and that the world culture at present is currently more caught up in such a way of thinking and being. The yin or ascending progression represents a more spiritual direction.[7]

If this assertion is correct, then it behoves women to look at the characteristics of both the descending and ascending numbers ascribed to their natal year. I believe that it may just be that as a woman becomes more self-actualized, the ascending or yin scale numbers ascribed to her natal year may be more activated and more relevant to her life. At the same time, because I and other Nine Star Ki practitioners have found that the descending (yang) natal number progression through time works for both men and women, in all examples and cases given, the yang progression has been used for both men and women throughout this book. I am inclined to believe that, if there is value in the ascending numbers and their associated energetics for women, women must address and work through the descending (yang) numbers and energetics in their lives first. At some other point, perhaps, the reverse will also be true. That is, that in times when spirituality becomes more dominant, men who would normally look to the descending (yang) progression, will need to attune themselves to the yin order.

Although the descending (yang) natal number progression is easy to calculate mathematically with the given formula, this is not so for the yin pattern. To make calculations easier and avoid confusion for everyone, a chart for a significant part of this era and the future using the yin or ascending natal number progressions for both years and months is presented here (Figures 29, 30 and 31).

Year	Number	Year	Number	Year	Number	Year	Number
1896	1	1925	3	1954	5	1983	7
1897	2	1926	4	1955	6	1984	8
1898	3	1927	5	1956	7	1985	9
1899	4	1928	6	1957	8	1986	1
1900	5	1929	7	1958	9	1987	2
1901	6	1930	8	1959	1	1988	3
1902	7	1931	9	1960	2	1989	4
1903	8	1932	1	1961	3	1990	5
1904	9	1933	2	1962	4	1991	6
1905	1	1934	3	1963	5	1992	7
1906	2	1935	4	1964	6	1993	8
1907	3	1936	5	1965	7	1994	9
1908	4	1937	6	1966	8	1995	1
1909	5	1938	7	1967	9	1996	2
1910	6	1939	8	1968	1	1997	3
1911	7	1940	9	1969	2	1998	4
1912	8	1941	1	1970	3	1999	5
1913	9	1942	2	1971	4	2000	6
1914	1	1943	3	1972	5	2001	7
1915	2	1944	4	1973	6	2002	8
1916	3	1945	5	1974	7	2003	9
1917	4	1946	6	1975	8	2004	1
1918	5	1947	7	1976	9	2005	2
1919	6	1948	8	1977	1	2006	3
1920	7	1949	9	1978	2	2007	4
1921	8	1950	1	1979	3	2008	5
1922	9	1951	2	1980	4	2009	6
1923	1	1952	3	1981	5	2010	7
1924	2	1953	4	1982	6	2011	8

Figure 29. Years and the yin, or ascending, year numbers

When your Nine Star Ki Birth Year Number is . . .				For birthdays between
Your Nine Star Ki Birth Month Number is . . .	7	4	1	4 Feb–5 Mar
	8	5	2	6 Mar–4 Apr
	9	6	3	5 Apr–5 May
	1	7	4	6 May–5 Jun
	2	8	5	6 Jun–7 Jul
	3	9	6	8 Jul–7 Aug
	4	1	7	8 Aug–7 Sep
	5	2	8	8 Sep–8 Oct
	6	3	9	9 Oct–7 Nov
	7	4	1	8 Nov–7 Dec
	8	5	2	8 Dec–5 Jan
	9	6	3	6 Jan–3 Feb

Figure 30 Months and yin, or ascending, natal month numbers

| Approximate dates | In the year | | | 24 Seasons |
	1,4,7	2,5,8	3,6,9	
22 Dec–5 Jan	5	2	8	(1) Winter solstice
6 Jan–3 Feb	6	3	9	(2) little cold (3) severe cold
4 Feb–5 Mar	7	4	1	(4) spring begins (5) rain water
6 Mar–4 Apr	8	5	2	(6) excited insects (7) vernal equinox
5 Apr–5 May	9	6	3	(8) clear and bright (9) grain rains
6 May–5 Jun	1	7	4	(10) summer begins (11) grain fills
6 Jun–7 Jul	2	8	5	(12) grain in ears (13) summer solstice
8 Jul–7 Aug	3	9	6	(14) slight heat (15) great heat
8 Aug–7 Sep	4	1	7	(16) autumn begins (17) limit of heat
8 Sep–8 Oct	5	2	8	(18) white dew (19) autumnal equinox
9 Oct–7 Nov	6	3	9	(20) cold dew (21) hoar frost descends
8 Nov–7 Dec	7	4	1	(22) winter begins (23) little snow
8 Dec–21 Dec	8	5	2	(24) heavy snow

Figure 31.
Ascending natal
month numbers
according to the
twenty-four season
concept.

5 ◆ Group Energetic Evaluation Chart

Number	1	2	3	4
Managing skills	**YIN – Allocator –** containing, storing, delineating boundaries, managing resources **YANG – Motivator –** generating, energizing, providing direction, reflection	**Supporter** sustaining, supporting, retaining, assimilating, anchoring, centring	**Planner** mapping, visioning, defining borders, strategizing, adapting, organizing	**Decision-Maker** clarifying, individuating, scheduling, initiating conflict, structuring
Persons involved				
Strategy				
No. 1 **Support for adult activation**	**Metal/Air Action –** provide historical data, provide summations, get No. 1 to consider the broader social implications, provide space for reflection and response, fatherly support	**Fire Action –** be direct, be convincing, promote excitement, be joyful, overcome anxieties, demonstrate appreciation, find out what else they need, sell them the idea	**Water Action –** communicate general trends of situation, delineate boundaries for person, energize them to move in given direction, be a well-spring, gentle action with reserve	Same as 3 tree/space but appeal to their maturity and sense to see things clearly. Support in prioritizing
No. 2 **Enhance to move person out of child activation**	Strategy No. 1 followed by **Tree/Space action –** be enthusiastic, show them what potential there is, let them know where things need to go, ask for their energy and gleanings from their reflections	Strategy No. 1 followed by **Metal/Air Action –** monitor quality, make them accountable, ask for progress reports, be accepting of what's offered, show social/historical importance of work done	Strategy No. 1 followed by **Fire Action –** show them what is possible, weave them into a greater plan or network of people, be enthusiastic, clarify their ideas	Same as Strategy No. 1 for 3 tree/space, but make sure that encouragement allows them to stick to one direction and within time limits set
No. 3 **Control inappropriate child action**	**Earth Action –** ground them, listen to them. Get details from them regarding vague fears. Acknowledge but challenge hesitancy	**Tree/Space Action –** clarify person's situation, initiate conflict if necessary, restructure person's situation, define limits, prioritize	**Metal/Air Action –** make person accountable, spell it out, establish order in their activity, list consequences, refer to team commitment, social order, morality, avoid direct confrontation	Same as 3 tree/space in Strategy No. 3, but over-ride their muddledness. Overcome confusion by refining, giving a clear evaluation of the situation, bringing balance to their perspective

5	6	7	8	9
Consolidator catalysing, leading, sorting, critiquing, also traits for 2 and 8	**Inspirer** equilibrating, resonating, receiving, balancing, establishing order	**Evaluator** accounting, refining, eliminating, evolving, managing change, quality control	**Producer** nurturing, transporting, supporting, producing, attention to details, integrating	**YIN – Sorter –** selling, problem solving, discriminating, transforming and Networker – team building, socializing, atmosphere builder **YANG – Coordinator –** coordinating, defining roles, directing, cooperation-building, and **Communicator –** appreciating, creating trust, expressing protecting
Fire Action – same as for 2 earth, but here over-ride indecisiveness, appeal to intellect, stimulate catalysing nature, define role, create trust, be supportive	**Earth Action –** nurture, provide adequate details, be an anchor, listen	Same as Strategy No. 1 for 6 metal, but more anchoring and centering, offer positive criticism, help to sustain momentum	Same as Strategy No. 1 for 2 and 5 earth, but help person to relax more, provide enthusiasm, lightness, and clarity, help with discrimination and priority	**Tree/Space Action –** provide ideas, give vision, enthusiasm and excitement, stimulate, map the territory to be explored, provide supportive muscle, create context
Same as Strategy No. 1 in 2 earth, followed by **Metal/Air Action –** critically weigh up options, help person adjust to change, establish order, encourage person to produce results, balance action	Strategy No. 1 followed by **Water Action –** reflect back, be receptive, manage resources, overcome rigidity by providing larger perspective	Strategy No. 1 followed by **Water Action –** as with 6 metal but here be more conservative, provide more direction, facilitate more truthful responses	Strategy No. 1 followed by **Metal/Air Action –** help to eliminate excess, refine, help person to focus beyond task, engage in play	Strategy No. 1 followed by **Earth Action –** get it all focused, encourage to act, spell out the end product, encourage diligence, provide realistic outlook and expectations, help person to match talk and actions
As Strategy No. 3 for 2 earth, getting person to commit themselves, over-ride sentimentality, encourage independence, provide time limits, give commands, help person to vision	**Fire Action –** spell it out, challenge dualistic (blank/white) thinking, overcome arrogance, clear air before grudges are set	**Fire Action –** don't buy smooth talk, challenge sense of entitlement, overcome any melancholy, keep person task-focused, appeal to social values and importance of the team	**Tree/Space Action –** snap person out of wallowing or hopelessness, encourage independent thinking, provide vision, even reframe structure, provide time frames	**Water Action –** listen, provide reflection, express caution, demand focus and direction, challenge flamboyance, facilitate direct communication, point out possible undertones

6 ◆ Calculation Formula for Years Beginning with 2000 CE

Whereas in the twentieth century, the formula for working out the numbers is to add the last two digits of the year, reduce it to a single digit, and then subtract from 10, from the year 2000 CE, these numbers will be subtracted from the number 9.

For example, for the year 2013, take the last two digits, 1 and 3, and add them together to give 4. Subtract 4 from 9 and you end up with 5, the natal year number for 2013.

But what if the last two digits add up to 9? It is very simple. Let's take the year 2018. The last two digits, 1 and 8 add up to 9. Subtract this 9 from 9 and you end up with 0. *Every time the numbers yield 0, this should be read as a 9 year.* Thus 2018 is a 9 year.

Notes

1. *The Ki*, pp. 3–5.

2. *The Astrology of I Ching*, p. 11.

3. *Chinese Astrology*, p. 48.

4. *Acupuncture and the Philosophy of the Far East*, p. 57.

5. *An Anthology of I Ching*, p. 87.

6. *An Anthology of I Ching*, p. 77.

7. *Nine Star Ki*.

Bibliography

Gagne, Stephen and Mann, John. *The Nine Ki Handbook*, Spiral-bound Books, Rochester, 1984

Hersey, Paul and Blanchard, Kenneth. *Management of Organizational Behavior*, Prentice Hall, Englewood Cliffs, NJ, 1982.

Kushi, Michio and Esko, Edward. *Nine Star Ki*, One Peaceful World Press, Becket, Massachusetts, 1991.

Muramoto, Naboru. *Healing Ourselves*, London, Michael Dempsey, 1975.

Ohsawa, George. *Acupuncture and the Philosophy of the Far East*, Tao Publications, Boston, Massachusetts, 1973.

Sherrill, W. A. and Chu, W. K. *An Anthology of I Ching*, Routledge & Kegan Paul, London, 1985.

Sherrill, W. A. and Chu, W. K. *The Astrology of I Ching*, Samual Weiser, York Beach, Maine, 1980.

Taguchi, Sinda. *Bai Hwa Zhong-guo Qi Xue Ming Li Ru Men*, Tokyo edition: B. Sunday, Publishing, 1984.

Tara, William. Macrobiotics and Human Behavior, Japan Publishing, Tokyo, New York, 1985.

Tulku, Tarthang. *Knowledge of Freedom*, Dharma Publishing, Berkeley, 1984.

Walters, Derek. *Chinese Astrology*, Aquarian Press, Wellingborough, Northants, 1987.

Wilheim, Richard and Baynes, Cary, F., editors. *The I Ching*, Routledge & Kegan Paul, London, 1975.

Yamamoto, Shizuko. *Barefoot Shiatsu*, Japan Publishing Inc., Tokyo.

Yoshikawa, Takashi. *The Ki*, St. Martin's Press, New York, 1986.

Glossary

Adult Number or adult natal year numbers: The number associated with the transformation dominant in the year that a person was born. It represents a person's self-actualizing potential.

Child Number or child natal month numbers: The number associated with the transformation dominant in the month that a person was born. Stress is more often that not associated with this number. It represents conditioning that a person experiences in their struggle to self-actualize or become more independent.

I Ching: An ancient Chinese divination system. Symbols of the I Ching are hexagrams derived from the trigram line markings that appeared on a tortoise in ancient times. To work the I Ching, a person asks a question and then performs certain ritual procedures in order to arrive at a hexagram which answers the question in the most auspicious way.

Ki: A Japanese term for life force; the same as *ch'i* (Chinese), *lung* (Tibetan) and *prana* (Sanskrit)

Ko Cycle: One of the Laws of Five Transformations, having to do with the way certain transformations control others when there are major disturbances in the life process. It is also called the cycle of death because as all things die, the order in which the organs or systems associated with certain transformations break down is in this particular order.

Lamaistic: 'Lama' means meditation master in Tibetan. In this context the term refers to an association with Tibetan Buddhist tradition in a monastic setting.

Law of Five Transformations: Guidelines discovered in ancient times which identify the factors and energetics that arise from the birth-to-death cycle of all phenomena.

Magic Square: Also referred to as Universal Chart. Originally found on Wu of Hsia's tortoise and thus considered a sign from divine forces. It represents the qualities, order, and movement of all phenomena here on earth as expressed in the Law of Five Transformations. Each of nine blocks in the magic square is a 'house' which bears certain qualities. This square is the cornerstone of Nine Star Ki astrology as it is used in China, Tibet and Japan.

Mother–Son: One of the Laws of Five Transformations where there is an intimate and direct relationship between two transformations. This relationship can be supportive, excessive, non-nurturing or depleting in nature.

Transformation: An aggregate of specific characteristics that is inclusive, but falls within a continuum. Originally, the translation of the Chinese for this term was 'element' as there is a kind of building-block quality. However, the term did not convey the dynamic quality of the aggregates, hence modern theorists have chosen 'transformation' as the term most suitable.

Trigram: A shorthand way of conveying certain qualities in nature, somewhat like calligraphy. Originally the line markings that are the trigrams were said to have appeared on a tortoise in antiquity.

Universal Charts: *see* Magic Square

Yang: A force in nature which exhibits contraction as a primary characteristic. Often associated with masculine energy.

Yin: A force in nature which exhibits expansiveness as a primary characteristic. Often associated with feminine energy.

Index

People interested in studying Nine Star Ki or receiving an astrological consultation for themselves, others or groups should contact Bob Sachs at:

DIAMOND WAY HEALTH ASSOCIATES
214 Girard Blvd. NE
Albuquerque, NM 87106
Telephone (505)265–4826

For courses on Oriental philosophy, healing, Macrobiotics, advanced studies in I Ching, and Nine Star Ki contact:

KUSHI INSTITUTE INTERNATIONAL
62 Buckminster Road
Brookline, MA. 02146

Melanie + Robert Sachs.
Diamond Way Ayurveda.
PO Box 13753
San Luis Obispo
CA 93406.

800 484 6283 Ex 7816
Tel. Fax 805 543 9291.